7 Tragic (Legal) Mistakes That Can Get Your Bank Accounts Frozen By The FTC, Leaving You Penniless…

And How To Protect Yourself, Your Family and Your Assets!

Chip Cooper, Esq.
Internet Attorney

7 Tragic (Legal) Mistakes That Can Get Your Bank Accounts Frozen By The FTC Leaving You Penniless...

Dedication

This book is dedicated to all Internet marketers and online entrepreneurs who've decided that FTC compliance is just as critical to their long term success as their marketing plan.

May your success inspire others to follow your lead!

And…

To Cathy, my wife and partner for her support and love, and for many years of putting up with me!

Mission Statement

- To *empower* you with a Simple Online Legal Solution…

- so you can be as successful as you want, and to grow your online businesses, as fast as you want…

- with the *confidence* that you're as legally protected as the Big Boys who can afford to hire expensive law firms,

- but without the high cost!

Please Review This Book

If this book opens your eyes to tragic legal mistakes that you absolutely, positively need to avoid, chances are this information would be valuable to your friends and colleagues as well.

So, do everyone a favor and review this book on Amazon.com!

You may also like or review it on Facebook, Google+, Twitter, and other social networks.

Thanks for your time and attention, and best of luck as you travel the road to online success!

Download FREE Blueprint

For a quick start to protecting your personal assets, download my Website Legal Compliance Blueprint.

www.ftcguardian.com/blueprint

ISBN-13: 9781502481283

ISBN-10: 1502481286

Copyright 2014 Chip Cooper. All rights reserved worldwide. No part of this work may be reprinted, copied, reproduced, or transmitted in any form or by any means without the prior written permission of the author.

Published in the United States of America

Disclaimer

THIS MATERIAL IS PROVIDED FOR EDUCATIONAL AND INFORMATIVE PURPOSES ONLY.

THIS INFORMATION DOES NOT CONSTITUTE LEGAL ADVICE, AND SHOULD NOT BE CONSTRUED AS SUCH.

TIPS AND STRATEGIES ARE PRESENTED BASED ON GENERAL INFORMATION AND NOT DESIGNED FOR SPECIFIC REQUIREMENTS OF ANY SPECIFIC ONLINE BUSINESS.

Contents

Foreward By Allyn Cutts
.... 11

**You're At Risk of Getting Your
Bank Accounts Frozen!**
.... 15

What Does This Mean To You?
.... 19

Tragic Mistake 1
Failure To Follow Online Advertising Laws
And Truth In Advertising
.... 29

Tragic Mistake 2
Failure To Follow the FTC Disclosure
Rules For Testimonials
.... 57

Tragic Mistake 3
You Offer A Biz Op Without Compliance
With FTC Regulations
.... 69

Tragic Mistake 4
Failure To Provide The Required Disclosures
For Your Membership Website
.... 77

Tragic Mistake 5
Failure to Honor Your Privacy Policy &
Make the Required Remarketing Disclosures
.... 85

Tragic Mistake 6
Failure to Manage Rogue Affiliates Who Get You
Sued For Their Deceptive Marketing Practices
.... 109

Tragic Mistake 7
Your Social Media Giveaways Get You Sued
For Running an Illegal Lottery
.... 117

**What Are Your Options for A Real Legal Solution
You Can Actually Have Confidence In?**
.... 127

Conclusion
.... 135

Appendices

Tragic Mistakes That Didn't Make The Top 7 List
.... 137

Appendix 1
FTC Accelerates Crackdown
On Fake News Sites
.... 139

Appendix 2
Blockbuster FTC Settlement!
Jesse Willms Agrees To $359 Million
Settlement For Deceptive Marketing Practice Claims
.... 143

Appendix 3
FTC's Settlement With Google
Provides Game Changing Internet
Privacy Regulations
....……..… 149

Appendix 4
The FTC Begins Crackdown
On Behavioral Ads - Is Your Site
In The Cross Hairs?
....…............ 153

About Chip Cooper, Esq.
....…..................... 157

7 Tragic (Legal) Mistakes That Can Get Your Bank Accounts Frozen By The FTC Leaving You Penniless...

Foreward By C. Allyn Cutts

Glad to know you have picked up Chip's book, because if you own a business and you have any type of website, this book could keep you out of a lot of trouble. It's the cheapest business insurance you can buy.

I have been in business for 30 years and have coached or consulted with hundreds of clients over the years, and if there is one theme that runs through most of them it's this... they don't take the time to truly understand the consequences of their actions, or lack of action when it comes to developing their website or online business.

As President and CEO of the Cutts Group, a Premier Marketing Service & Reputation Management Agency in the US, it's our job to help our clients grow their business legally and ethically by developing strategies that drives more qualified visitors to their website, through their front-door, and make their phone ring, while protecting their online reputation.

In the 'old-days', prior to 2003, it pretty much seemed like when it came to having a business online and online marketing - there were basically no rules...

All that has changed!

7 Tragic (Legal) Mistakes That Can Get Your Bank Accounts Frozen By The FTC Leaving You Penniless...

I personally know several business owners who have run into legal trouble with the FTC, and have since read or heard of many more businesses who have run afoul with the FTC since 2003. And I can tell you this, without a shadow-of-doubt, you will not win a case against the FTC.

Just ask Google.

So, today a day does not go by that we don't first ask new clients if they have consulted with an Internet attorney and understand the 'Rules of the Road', before we start to work on their business.

If the answer is 'No', we always advise that they either hire a top Internet attorney like Chip, or get a service like FTCGuardian.com.

I first met Chip in 2012 at a meeting in New York where 25 or so top-level online marketers were gathering to discuss online tips, tricks, and strategies to grow our businesses. There were two attorneys in the room, an IP attorney and Chip Cooper, an Internet attorney.

Chip listened to us talk all weekend about all the stuff we were doing online, the little strategies we were using or developing online, the way we were growing our businesses, and the money we were making...
Then on the last day, Chip presented his *'Rules of the Road'* presentation, and to be perfectly honest, most of us really weren't that interested in listening to an attorney preach about all this legal compliance stuff. After all, most of us had been fairly successful online and offline and never had any real legal issues. Maybe we had just been lucky, I don't know.

Later, Chip and I ended up having dinner together and spending some time together. Over dinner we discussed my business and the type of work we do for our clients and all that, then the conversation shifted to the legal documents on our website, and on our clients' websites.

Chip asked where I got our website legal document... I think he had a pretty good idea what I was going to say. I explained I'd been online a long time, and had just picked up templates or borrowed legal documents from others I knew online, and basically just made a few changes here and there and threw them up.

What came next changed everything... Little did I know the risks I had been taking with my business, and family finances. We file and pay our corporate taxes, pay our business license fees, you name it - I thought we were solid. Besides, Cutts Group is fully a incorporated entity, my family finances and property are protected. Not!

When Chip started punching holes in our online legal documents, taking stabs at our affiliate agreements, and other documents we were using, and some that we should have been using, and we weren't... I was floored.

Chip explained that if a business falls into the FTC crosshairs, there's no corporate veil, the FTC can freeze your business and personal bank accounts, as well as seize your personal property and your spouse's property. There's not a prayer in the world that can help you. OUCH!

Needless to say, I now have religion when it comes to online compliance, and understanding the *Rules of the Road and his Easy-To-Understand Strategies.*

Chip Cooper has changed how I think about the compliance side of our business, and our clients' properties, and I'm extremely thankful for that.

Basically, this book is a list of what Chip calls the top **7 Tragic (Legal) Mistakes** a business online can make.

If I can offer a recommendation to anyone who wishes to succeed online, it's to read this book and carefully follow what Chip Cooper has to say.

You should also take advantage of Chip's FREE download: Website Legal Compliance Blueprint – www.ftcguardian.com/blueprint

You're At Risk Of Getting Your Bank Accounts Frozen!

That's right.

Think about it for a minute.

You're at your desk at the beginning of your work day. Drinking your first cup of coffee.

You're working on your online business.

There's a knock on the door. It's the local process server with a pile of paper from the FTC naming you as a defendant for a deceptive marketing practice.

You're now a "Defendant". It's hard to actually say the word. And the United States Government, with all its resources to wage war against you, is suing you.

This isn't a warning. It's the real thing! Something you've hardly even considered before. Now it's a reality.

You can't believe it. Why me?

7 Tragic (Legal) Mistakes That Can Get Your Bank Accounts Frozen By The FTC Leaving You Penniless...

After all, you're ethical. And you know other marketers who have done the same thing, or maybe much more than you. You always thought one of them would get into trouble with the FTC, but not YOU!

What to do? How do I find an attorney to represent me? Can I afford the massive legal fees? Not to mention the massive disruption to your life. And time away from your business!

The phone rings. It's your banker. "Sorry, I've had to freeze your bank accounts by an order from the FTC."

Now, the initial shock gives way to the reality of this development.

How do I pay the bills? The mortgage? I can't even go the to instant banker and withdraw cash!

And, how do I break the news to my spouse?

This story isn't as far-fetched as you may think. It's real. It can happen to you.

And the longer you continue to grow your online business, the greater the likelihood that it WILL happen to you. That is, unless you decide to learn – and follow – some of the basic steps to protect yourself.

The Federal Trade Commission (FTC) enforces the Rules and Regulations that govern unfair and deceptive marketing practices in the USA. If you don't know them, if you don't adhere to them, you do so at your own risk.

7 Tragic Legal Mistakes That Can Get Your Bank Accounts Frozen By The FTC Leaving You Penniless...

Plus, there are laws that are not new, but they're not well known by most Internet marketers and online entrepreneurs. And they apply to your online business.

The scary thing is… these little known laws can have devastating effects if you don't know how they apply to your online business. And know how to avoid their devastating consequences.

If you've been around for a while, you probably know that The "Wild, Wild West" ended in 2009. That's when the tsunami of new laws and regulations affecting websites started.

During the "Wild, Wild, West" days, the buzz was about what color hat you were wearing as an Internet marketer or online entrepreneur.

- White Hat: you were completely ethical in your marketing practices.

- Black Hat: you used marketing practices that were considered by most to be unethical.

- Grey Hat: you used both White Hat practices and Black Hat marketing practices.

It's vastly different now. And it'll never be the same!

The color of your hat doesn't mean much if the FTC comes knocking at your door!

7 Tragic (Legal) Mistakes That Can Get Your Bank Accounts Frozen By The FTC Leaving You Penniless...

What Does This Mean to You?

(Hint - You'd Better Adapt Now, or Risk Losing Your Business!)

(It's Not The Color of Your Hat Anymore!)

For starters, it means that the color of your hat is just that... old hat!

Today, it's about legal compliance (not your hat color). These are now the critical questions you must ask yourself:
- Is my website legal, and

- Are my marketing practices legal?

You And Everyone Online Is Now on the FTC's Radar 24x7!

And it also means that the Federal Trade Commission (FTC) is now on the warpath with new regulations and aggressive enforcement.

Just take a look at a few recent cases:

- **$250,000** - 2011 - Learning Systems – affiliate marketers falsely posed as consumers & reviewers.

7 Tragic (Legal) Mistakes That Can Get Your Bank Accounts Frozen By The FTC Leaving You Penniless...

- **$500,000** - 2011 - 10 websites – fake news and consumer testimonials.

- **$350 Million** - 2012 - Jesse Willms – free offers and recurring billing plans.

- **$18 Million** – 2012 – Commerce Planet - free offers and recurring billing plan

- **$2.9 Million** – 2014 - Online Entrepreneur, Inc. d/b/a The Six Figure Program - sale of fraudulent business opportunity in violation of the FTC's Business Opportunity Rule

- **Assets Frozen In Pending Case** (Damages To Be Determined) – 2014 – Apply Knowledge – work at home coaching programs

And State Attorneys General are also bringing suits against marketers based on "Little FTC Acts" that are similar to the U.S. FTC Act. In 2013, the Attorney General for the State of New York sued Trump University for **$40 million**. The suit alleged that Trump University was engaging in deceptive practices with its real estate courses that were useless seminars, coaching, mentorships, and upsells, all promising to make students rich, but really didn't.

One significant take-away from these cases and others is this: generally speaking, the marketing practices in these cases are the same marketing practices all Internet marketers and online entrepreneurs use:

- squeeze pages,
- testimonials for social proof,

- free offers,
- upsells,
- downsells,
- one-time offers,
- contests,
- social media promotions
- retargeting,
- memberships and continuity plans, and
- and affiliate marketing partners.

The catch is that they were used *deceptively (and therefore illegally)*, according to the FTC, and therefore they became targets aggressively pursued by the FTC.

Deceptive practices can take many forms, such as:

- unsubstantiated claims,

- false promises,

- incomplete descriptions,

- false testimonials or comparisons,

- small-print qualifications of advertisements, and

- partial disclosure, or visual distortion of products.

Sometimes, deceptive practices are no-brainers, meaning they are clearly deceptive, and there's no excuse or defense for these practices.

In other cases, however, the distinction may not as clear.

And in some, there may even be legal agreements that disclose material terms of offers, but the terms and conditions are not presented properly according to the FTC.

The result: huge fines, and other restrictions on future marketing practices.

What is The FTC's Legal Authority Anyway?

The FTC was created by the U.S. Congress in 1914. The FTC is the federal consumer protection agency charged with safeguarding consumers against *"unfair and deceptive trade practices,"* according to Section 5 of the Federal Trade Commissions Act.

States have similar laws and regulations, but the primary focus is on the FTC.

The FTC's mission covers wide areas, including false advertising, product warranties, product labeling and packaging, lending, fair credit billing and reporting and telemarketing. These areas, however, aren't the ones that directly affect you.

The big areas that directly affect you and your lists are the FTC rules regarding privacy, data security, and online marketing practices, particularly:

- how you collect, use, and share information, and

- how you sell your products, services and information.

What Does The FTC Consider as "Deceptive" or "Unfair"?

In order to understand what the FTC believes is a "deceptive" or "unfair" act or practice, the best place to begin is with ad claims and business practices, because they are the key things the FTC focuses on.

> **Tip:** In a nutshell, a *business practice* is a practice and/or procedure used by a business to achieve its goals.

There will be more on ad claims in the Tragic Mistake 1 chapter, but for now the following tip will suffice.

> **Tip:** In a nutshell, an *ad claim* is a statement regarding the performance, features and/or benefits of a product or service that is intended to persuade a consumer to respond favorably to a call to action. The call to action is what you want the prospect to do – opt in to your squeeze page, sign up for a webinar, provide information, take a survey, or purchase a product or service.

So, what makes a business practice or ad claim "deceptive" or "unfair" according to the FTC?

The FTC says that a claim is "deceptive" if it:

- is likely to mislead consumers acting reasonably under the circumstances; and

- is "material" - that is, important to a consumer's decision to buy or use the product or service.

The FTC says that a claim or business practice is "unfair" if it:

- causes or is likely to cause substantial consumer injury which a consumer could not reasonably avoid; and

- is not outweighed by the benefit to consumers.

These are the general principles followed by the FTC.

They're important only as beginning points.

> **Tip**: What you really need to understand is how these principles are applied to the specific marketing practices you undertake every day.

> **Tip**: And also, very important, is how you use your lists – specifically, how you use and share the personal information, and other privacy-protected information, in your lists.

How does the FTC determine if you're engaged in "deceptive" or "unfair" practices?

- The FTC's review focuses on what a <u>reasonable consumer</u> would think. Everything is considered – words, phrases, images, videos, slogans – to determine how a consumer would view what it conveys.

- The FTC would consider what is stated and not stated. For example, what you actually say or do, and what is implied by what you say or do. You're required to have substantiation (or proof) that you can back up your claims.

- Then the FTC considers if what you say and do would be material, or important, to a typical consumer regarding whether to act on your call to action.

The FTC Can Freeze Your Bank Accounts

Engaging in "deceptive" claims or "unfair" practices can have massive consequences on your online business, your profits, and your family – and they're all bad!

The FTC's remedies include:

- Cease and Desist Orders – legally binding orders to stop the deceptive ad or practice.

- Corrective Ads – requirements to conduct new, corrective ad campaigns to correct the deceptive ad or unfair practice.

- Civil Penalties (Fines) – these can range from thousands to millions of dollars, and could wipe out your online business in a single day.

- Freezing Your Bank Accounts!

> **Tip** – The FTC's authority is very broad. The FTC can even *freeze your bank and PayPal accounts*! To most marketers, this is the scariest FTC remedy of all.

The FTC's Website Complaint Form

And here's another take-away that you should be aware of.

This one's big, very big. It could transform your life.

You probably know that the FTC has a website. What you may not know is that on this website they have a complaint form, and it's really very easy to find. All anyone has to do is to search online for "FTC Complaint" and it'll show up as no. 1.

So, you now understand why it's really easy for anyone with a complaint with the FTC - and all it takes is just one:

- a disgruntled customer,
- a privacy activist,
- your competitor…

to file a complaint against you that may very well *transform* you from being on the FTC radar (which all Internet

7 Tragic Legal Mistakes That Can Get Your Bank Accounts Frozen By The FTC Leaving You Penniless...

marketers and online entrepreneurs are) – to being on the FTC's target list.

Believe me, this is the last place you want to find yourself.

> **Tip:** Don't be fooled into thinking that you're too small to be a target by the FTC. The FTC Complaint Form is available for anyone to file a complaint at any time.

And you should understand that even beginners (and maybe you) are potential targets; it only takes a single disgruntled customer clicking on that FTC form to transform your life.

But it's even more important to understand this - as you become successful, and grow your business, you'll become even more of an *inviting potential target* for anyone who might want to file an FTC complaint or take some kind of legal action against you.

Now that the "Wild, Wild West" is over, a real, valid, honest-to-goodness *legal solution* is now just as essential, just as important, as your:

- shopping cart,
- email autoresponder, and
- email list.

Personal Asset Protection Won't Work Against The FTC

Another thing... you may not realize it, but your personal assets are at risk. That's right, your non-business assets and those of <u>your family</u>.

> **Warning:** Regardless of how many legal entities you set up for purposes of personal asset protection, the FTC can go right through these barriers like a hot knife through butter!

So, what to do?

First, you should focus on the Top 7 Tragic (Legal) Mistakes discussed this book!

These are the BIG ONES – the really big Mistakes - that you absolutely, positively need to understand and avoid.

At all costs!

There are some other Tragic Mistakes in the Appendices. They are all important, but they didn't make the cut for the Top 7 list.

> **Tip:** Bottom line, if you're serious about succeeding with your online business, you need to adapt to the new legal landscape on the Web. *Ignorance of the law is no excuse!*

Tragic Mistake 1

Failure To Follow Online Advertising Laws And Truth In Advertising

What Is False Advertising?

In short, false advertising consists of an ad claim that is either –

- literally false, or
- is likely to mislead, deceive, or confuse consumers.

What's an Ad Claim?

This is the way the FTC defines "ad claim":

- a statement regarding the performance, features and/or benefits of a product or service,
- that is intended to persuade a consumer to respond favorably to a call to action (CTA).

The CTA is what you want the prospect to do – optin on your squeeze page, sign up for a webinar, provide information, take a survey, or purchase a product or service.

An ad claim is an explicit *or implicit* statement that a product or service has a feature or benefit. Implied claims are held to the same standard as explicit claims.

Tip: The key to evaluating an ad claim is the *net impression* conveyed by all elements of the claim, including the text and context of the ad, name of product or service, labels, and surrounding images.

That's pretty basic stuff.

What's an Earnings Claim?

The FTC also has a definition for a special type of ad claim known as an "earnings claim" which relates to products or services that show consumers how to make money or promise a financial benefit.

This is how the FTC defines "earnings claim":

- An oral, written, or visual representation

- That states a specific level of potential sales, income, gross or net profit, or

- Facts which *suggest* a specific level of the above.

Examples of facts *suggesting* a specific level of the above would include statements regarding future financial benefits when coupled with –

- *A photo of a marketer standing by a new Mercedes automobile (facts that suggest a specific level of financial benefit, i.e. sufficient to purchase a similar automobile);* and

- *Screen shots of the marketer's PayPal account showing a large number of sales transactions (facts that suggest a similar level of financial benefit).*

Tip: The important thing to remember here is that ad claims are regulated by the FTC. If the ad claim does not follow FTC rules, it gives the FTC grounds to file a lawsuit for false advertising.

It's important to distinguish an ad claim from "puffery".

Why is this important? The short answer is that "puffery" is not considered to be an ad claim. So, "puffery" is not regulated by FTC rules, and therefore can't be deceptive.

Tip: "Puffery" is always legal in all circumstances. And ad claims will not be legal if not properly substantiated. That's it. That's why it's important to have a clear understanding of what amounts to "puffery". Ad claims (if they amount to false advertising) can get you into big trouble with the FTC. Puffery can't.

What Is Puffery?

"Puffery" is a legal term for an exaggerated statement made for promotional purposes which states subjective rather objective views, and is so exaggerated that consumers are not likely to be mislead, deceived, or confused.

Two U.S. Circuit Courts of Appeals have defined puffery as "exaggerated advertising, blustering and boasting upon which no reasonable buyer would rely."

One of the keys for distinguishing a puffery statement from a regulated ad claim is whether the claim at issue –

- is quantifiable, and
- capable of being proven false using scientific methods.

Result - If it's quantifiable and capable of being proven false, then it's an ad claim (not puffery).

An Example of Puffery

A great example of puffery involves the claim made by Papa John's "Better Ingredients. Better Pizza."

In the case of *Pizza Hut, Inc. v Papa John's Intern., Inc.*, the 5th Circuit Court of Appeals found that the claim was puffery, not an ad claim. The Court found the claim to be the epitomy of puffery – boasting and exaggeration. In addition, the Court pointed out that the statement was generic in that it did not –

- identify any specifics regarding "better", and
- did not offer any comparison with a competitor's product.

It's also fair to conclude that the claim was not quantifiable, nor was it capable of being proven false using scientific methods.

What Is NAD?

NAD is an acronym that stands for the National Advertising Division of the Council of Better Business Bureaus.

NAD is a self-regulatory organization that reviews truth in advertising issues, specifically factual ad claims for accuracy.

NAD's decisions regarding advertising issues assist advertisers in evaluating their ad claims. Compliance with NAD's decisions in voluntary.

So, even though NAD decisions are voluntary, they should be given considerable weight in evaluation of ad claims, and ads that may be puffery.

Examples of NAD Decisions Re Puffery

Here is a collection of 4 NAD decisions that should provide some valuable insight regarding how to determine the difference between puffery and a regulated ad claim.

- Exaggeration/Boastful Statements – Issue is whether the statement can be proven true or false, or is it so vague that no one will treat it as factual –

  o Puffery:
    - "America's Favorite Pizza"
    - "America's Best Loved Coffee"
    - "The Earth's Most Comfortable Shoes"

  o Not Puffery (Regulated Ad Claim)
    - "The Antioxidant Superpower"
    - "Trusted By Moms"
    - "Leading Brand"

- Comparative Ad That Identifies Competitors – Issue is whether the statement identifies competitors or certain aspects of the competitor's products –

  o Puffery:
    - "Beech-Nut is a better choice"
  o Not Puffery (Regulated Ad Claim)
    - "Taste The Best at a Sensible Price" (when shown next to the competitor's products)

- Comparative Ad That Identifies Measurable Results – Issue is whether the advertiser claims superiority of a specific attribute of product –

- Puffery

    - "Better Ingredients. Better Pizza." (when no specific ingredients are identified)

- Not Puffery (Regulated Ad Claim)

    - "Tastes Most Like Butter Even Better"
    - "The best Compact Coffee Solution"
    - "Discover The Better Taste of Progresso"

- Statement Placed Near Product Performance or Disease Prevention Claims – Issue is whether the exaggerated claim is located close to other quantifiable claims –

    - Puffery

        - "World's Most Effective Energy Drinks" (placed on top of product website and not next to any performance claims of product)

    - Not Puffery (Regulated Ad Claim)

        - "Cheat Death", "Live Preserver", "The New Shape of Protection" (placed beside a statement describing the horrors of cancer)

(The foregoing analysis is based on an article by Gurnani, Abhishk K. and Talati, Ashish R., FDLI, "The World's Most Trusted Article on Puffery", American Bar Association, November/December, 2008.)

> **Tip:** If you're going to be aggressive with marketing statements, you should be careful to stay on the side of puffery. Don't cross the line to regulated ad claims. If you do cross the line, you'll be subject to the Prior Substantiation Rule.

Regulated Ad Claims – The Prior Substantiation Rule

The basic ideas is that if you make a regulated ad claim, then you must, *prior to disseminating the ad*, develop substantiation for the claim either by –
- scientific data, or
- results determined though consumer surveys.

> **Prior Substantiation Rule**: This is the FTC's statement of the prior substantiation rule taken from an actual case:
>
> "Before disseminating an advertisement, the advertiser must substantiate all claims – express and implied – that the ad conveys to reasonable consumers".

As discussed above, the Prior Substantiation Rule does *not* apply to puffery.

Back in 1984, the FTC issued a statement regarding its policy for prior substantiation of ad claims:

- "First, we reaffirm our commitment to the underlying legal requirement of advertising substantiation that advertisers and ad agencies have a **reasonable basis for advertising claims before they are disseminated**."

- "The Commission intends to continue vigorous enforcement of this existing legal requirement that advertisers substantiate express and implied claims, however conveyed, that make **objective assertions** about the item or service advertised."

- "Objective claims for products or services represent **explicitly** or by **implication** that the advertiser has a reasonable basis supporting these claims."

- "These representations of substantiation are material to consumers. That is, consumers would be less likely to rely on claims for products and services if they knew the advertiser did not have a reasonable basis for believing them to be true."

- "Therefore, a firm's failure to possess and rely upon a reasonable basis for objective claims constitutes an unfair and deceptive act or practice in violation of Section 5 of the Federal Trade Commission Act."

You should understand that the FTC often makes inquiries to advertisers in cases where the FTC wants to see prior substantiation. This inquiry may be made prior to filing a lawsuit.

The FTC may either initiate a –
- a compulsory inquiry by subpoena or civil investigation, or

- an informal information request seeking voluntary cooperation such as with the issuance of an "access letter".

After an investigation, if the FTC determines that there is "reason to believe" that the ad in question amounts to false advertising, the FTC may sue you – either by filing an administrative complaint or a complaint in a U.S. District Court. In both cases, the FTC has the burden of proving its false advertising allegations.

How To Substantiate Your Ad Claims

A detailed discussion of ad claim substantiation is beyond the scope of this book. However, the general principles discussed below should point you in the right direction.

Remember, both *direct* (absolute and express) claims and *implied* claims are required to be substantiated.

An example of an *implied* claim would be a claim using a comparative approach, such as "Better Than All The Rest" (implying that the product is better than the remainder of the specific products in the category).

Substantiation of these claims means the verification, confirmation, and evidence or proof that an ad claim is true. Consumers need to have confidence that an advertiser has a reasonable basis for making a claim.

Here are some examples of *direct* claims and the related challenges regarding substantiation and back-up:

- If you claim "We're No. 1", you need to be very specific regarding how you determine no. 1 – no. 1 at what? - in gross sales, in sales growth for a specific period, in the number of widgets sold?

- If you claim the "Latest And Greatest", "Next Generation" or words to that effect, you should substantiate how the claim is true – explain specifically how you justify the claim in relation to other competitive products on the market.

- If you claim "User Friendly" or "Easy-To-Use", you need to be specific regarding substantiation of specifically how much time a certain task routinely takes, exactly which steps are automated, etc.

For claims that advertise a *level of substantiation* – "Tests Prove" or "Studies Show" – you need at least the advertised level of substantiation.

For *scientific* claims – such as for weight loss or dietary supplements – the FTC requires "competent and reliable scientific evidence" including –

- Tests, analyses, research, studies, or other evidence based on the expertise of professionals in the relevant area,

- That have been conducted and evaluated in an objective manner by persons qualified to do so, and

- Using procedures generally accepted in the profession to yield accurate and reliable results

The following is *not* "competent" scientific evidence and/or does not constitute adequate substantiation:

- Anecdotal evidence *alone* from customers (for example, non-factual evidence based on the experiences of a few people, for example, a person tells how his breath feels fresher after using a certain brand of toothpaste); however, anectdotal evidence when coupled with a few well-controlled studies may be sufficient;

- Newspaper, magazine, or Wikipedia articles;

- Sales materials from the manufacturer;

- Low rate of product returns or money-back guarantee;

- Testimonials.

Testimonials Are Considered To Be Ad Claims

Testimonials are essentially the other side of the ad claim coin –

- Ad claims are made *by you*, the marketer about your products or services;

- Testimonials are made by others *for you* and your products and services.

The FTC has made it clear that testimonials and expert endorsements must be substantiated -

- as though they were made by the marketer itself, or

- be *properly disclaimed*.

A testimonial or endorsement must represent –

- the experience that is representative of a typical customer can expect with the product or service, or
- be *properly disclaimed*.
  - There is no exception for personal opinion of a person giving a testimonial.
  - The testimonial must give the honest opinions, findings, beliefs, or experience of the testimonials.
  - Any material connection between the testimonialist and the marketer must be disclosed (as discussed in the next chapter).

How To Make Sure Your Testimonials Are "Properly Disclaimed"

A clear and conspicuous disclaimer is required for testimonials that do not reflect experience that is representative of what a typical customer can expect.

An example of a proper disclaimer for a weight loss claim would be: "On Average, Users Reported Positive Effect After 12 Weeks of Use".

Vague, non-specific disclaimers won't work any more, such as –

- "Results Not Typical", or

- "Your Results May Vary".

Three quick and easy ways to get into trouble with deceptive testimonials –

- The testimonialist may not have experienced the reported result;

- The result may be attributable to other factors, such as (i) diet or exercise for weight loss, or (ii) prior experience with making money products;

- If a testimonial claims results that are not typical without a proper disclaimer.

- If the testimonialist falsely states or implies that he/she actually used the product or service.

Beware of Earnings Disclaimers!

Earnings disclaimers are commonly used to qualify earnings claims. Most earnings disclaimers may be boiled down to the these elements –

- No promise you will make money;

- No promise you will not lose money;

- Internet businesses are risky; and

- Seek professional advice before purchasing any money-making scheme.

The problem with the way many Earnings Disclaimers – and a serious trap for the unwary - is that they're offered to *contradict* earnings claims.

The FTC has made it very clear:

"[Disclaimers] should be presented clearly and conspicuously so that consumers can actually notice and understand it.... [A]dvertisers [cannot] use fine print to contradict other statements in an ad or to clear up misimpressions that the ad would leave otherwise."

The NAD also weighed in:

"While disclosures may be used in advertising to reduce the potential for consumer confusion, they cannot be used to change the express meaning of a claim or to render truthful an otherwise misleading advertising claim.

And the 3rd Circuit Court of Appeals added this:

"One cannot escape liability for a literally false claim by pointing to a later disclaimer."

7 Tragic (Legal) Mistakes That Can Get Your Bank Accounts Frozen By The FTC Leaving You Penniless...

> **Tip:** Be very careful to not fall into the trap of believing that you can promise the moon with earnings claims, and it will all be legal if you simply post an Earnings Disclaimer to your website. Your Earnings Disclaimer will *not* be effective to "sanitize" or cure an otherwise deceptive ad claim. And the FTC may also claim that your attempt to render a deceptive ad claim to be truthful with the Earnings Disclaimer is, itself, a deceptive marketing practice.

What To Do If You Use Experts As Endorsers

- You must provide the qualifications that support the expert's standing to be represented as an expert in the specific field of the endorsement.

- The expert must have a reasonable basis to provide the opinion expressed in the endorsement.

- The expert must actually use his/her expertise in evaluating the features or characteristics of the product or service.

- The features or characteristics featured in the endorsement must be relevant to an ordinary consumer's use of, or experience with, the product or service and which are also available to the ordinary consumer.

Ad Claims Come In All Shapes, Sizes, and Places

Don't be lulled into sleep by thinking that ad claims only appear on your website's sales pages.

7 Tragic Legal Mistakes That Can Get Your Bank Accounts Frozen By The FTC Leaving You Penniless...

Ad claims may appear in all shapes, sizes, and places. No matter what form the ad takes, the advertiser still must substantiate all ad claims before substantiation.

Ad claims may appear in other forms and places, such as:

- Website pages other than sales pages;
- Social media pages;
- Blogs;
- YouTube videos and other videos; and
- Contests (for example, an Oracle ad stating that its Exadata server is "5X Faster Than IBM... Or You Win $10,000,000").

Also, be very careful with these hazards –

- Website reviews posted by customers;
- Social media pages;
- Guarantees;
- "Free" trials where customers have to cancel within a stated time period or their credit cards will be charged.

> **Tip:** If you're not really sure about how to substantiate ad claims, the best approach is to clearly understand puffery, and then to always stay on the side of puffery without crossing the line to regulated ad claims.

How to Provide The Required Advertising Disclosures (2013)

The FTC says that an ad claim is "deceptive" if it:

- is likely to mislead consumers acting reasonably under the circumstances; and

- is "material" - that is, important to a consumer's decision to buy or use the product or service.

- So, for your ads to be <u>not deceptive</u>, you're required to disclose all material facts that are important to a consumer's decision to buy or use the product or service.

> **Tip** – The FTC believes that how and where these disclosures are made is an important factor in determining whether an ad claim is deceptive. The purpose of the .com Disclosures is to provide guidance regarding how to make these disclosures.

In 2013, the FTC issued revised .com Disclosures. It's purpose was to update the FTC's prior guidelines for disclosures regarding marketing and advertising on the Internet so that consumers could be protected from deceptive ads.

The FTC's .com Disclosures Apply To Anyone Engaged in Digital Advertising And Online Marketing

This means that big companies as well as solo entrepreneurs who operate a single ecommerce website are engaged in digital advertising and marketing, and therefore are subject to the guidelines of the .com Disclosures.

It's important to note that the .com Disclosures are not definitive law, meaning that they are guidelines. So, compliance is voluntary; however, if you engage in practices contrary to the .com Disclosures, particularly if consumers have sent complaints to the FTC or if there is a pattern of noncompliance, you may very well get the dreaded knock on your door from the FTC.

Tip: Despite the fact that the .com Disclosures are not definitive law, you need to understand them. The last thing you want to happen is for your customers to complain to the FTC about how they were confused about your pricing, or a required add-on, or some other aspect of your sales and marketing messages.

The .com Disclosures address many issues regarding disclosure placement that reflect the current Internet landscape –

- Social media, generally;
- Specific constraints of certain social media, for example the character limitations of Twitter;
- Automation of engagement on social media;
- Mobile apps, and particularly the space limitations of mobile device screens;
- Hashtags (#); and
- Linked disclosures on a website, just to name a few.

The bottom line is that the responsibility of the advertiser to ensure that –

- all providers, including their own website, social media platforms, blogs, or video platforms, are capable of including the appropriate disclosures, and
- in fact, do provide the appropriate disclosures.

.com Disclosures General Rules And Principles

The .com Disclosures provide the following *general rules*

stating that all disclosures should be –

- Proximate to the information so the consumer does not have to hunt for it;

- Of at least the same size as the message;

- In the same format as the message;

- Accessible on all platforms used; and

- Understandable by the consumer.

The .com Disclosures provide the following *5 general principles.*

1. The same consumer protection laws that apply to commercial activities in other media apply online, including activities in the mobile marketplace. The FTC Act's prohibition on "unfair or deceptive acts or practices" encompasses online advertising, marketing, and sales.

In addition, many Commission rules and guides are –

- not limited to any particular medium used to disseminate claims or advertising, and

- therefore, apply to the wide spectrum of online activities.

2. When practical, advertisers should incorporate relevant limitations and qualifying information –

- into the underlying claim,
- rather than having a separate disclosure qualifying the claim.

3. Required disclosures must be "clear and conspicuous."

In evaluating whether a disclosure is likely to be clear and conspicuous, advertisers should consider –

- its placement in the ad, and
- its proximity to the relevant claim.

The closer the disclosure is to the claim to which it relates, the better."

Additional considerations include:

- the prominence of the disclosure;
- whether it is unavoidable;
- whether other parts of the ad distract attention from the disclosure;
- whether the disclosure needs to be repeated at different places on a website;
- whether disclosures in audio messages are presented in an adequate volume and cadence; whether visual disclosures appear for a sufficient duration; and

- whether the language of the disclosure is understandable to the intended audience.

4. To make a disclosure clear and conspicuous, advertisers should:

- Place the disclosure as close as possible to the triggering claim.

- Take account of the various devices and platforms consumers may use to view advertising and any corresponding disclosure. If an ad is viewable on a particular device or platform, any necessary disclosures should be sufficient to prevent the ad from being misleading when viewed on that device or platform.

- When a space-constrained ad requires a disclosure, incorporate the disclosure into the ad whenever possible. However, when it is not possible to make a disclosure in a space-constrained ad, it may, under some circumstances, be acceptable to make the disclosure clearly and conspicuously on the page to which the ad links.

- When using a hyperlink to lead to a disclosure -

    o make the link obvious;

    o label the hyperlink appropriately to convey the importance, nature, and relevance of the information it leads to;

- o use hyperlink styles consistently, so consumers know when a link is available;

- o place the hyperlink as close as possible to the relevant information it qualifies and make it noticeable;

- o take consumers directly to the disclosure on the click-through page;

- o assess the effectiveness of the hyperlink by monitoring click-through rates and other information about consumer use and make changes accordingly.

- Preferably, design advertisements so that "scrolling" is not necessary in order to find a disclosure. When scrolling is necessary, use text or visual cues to encourage consumers to scroll to view the disclosure.

- Keep abreast of empirical research about where consumers do and do not look on a screen.

- Recognize and respond to any technological limitations or unique characteristics of a communication method when making disclosures.

- Display disclosures before consumers make a decision to buy – e.g. before they "Add To Cart". Also, recognize that disclosures may have to be repeated before purchase to ensure that they are adequately presented to consumers.

- Repeat disclosures, as needed, on lengthy websites and in connection with repeated claims. Disclosures may also have to be repeated if consumers have multiple routes through a website.

- If a product or service promoted online is intended to be (or can be) purchased from "brick and mortar" stores or from online retailers other than the advertiser itself, then any disclosure necessary to prevent deception or unfair injury should be presented in the ad itself – that is, before consumers head to a store or some other online retailer.

- Necessary disclosures should not be relegated to "terms of use" and similar contractual agreements.

- Prominently display disclosures so they are noticeable to consumers, and evaluate the size, color and graphic treatment of the disclosure in relation to other parts of the webpage.

- Review the entire ad to assess whether the disclosure is effective in light of other elements – text, graphics, hyperlinks, or sound – that might distract consumers' attention from the disclosure.

- Use audio disclosures when making audio claims, and present them in a volume and cadence so that consumers can hear and understand them.

- Display visual disclosures for a duration sufficient for consumers to notice, read and understand them.

- Use plain language and syntax so that consumers understand the disclosures.

5. If a disclosure is necessary to prevent an advertisement from being deceptive, unfair, or otherwise violative of a Commission rule,

- and it is not possible to make the disclosure clearly and conspicuously,

- then that ad should not be disseminated.

- This means that if a particular platform does not provide an opportunity to make clear and conspicuous disclosures, then that platform should not be used to disseminate advertisements that require disclosures.

Download the .com Disclosures

Probably the most informative aspect of the .com Disclosures are the examples provided.

The only way to review these examples is to download the .com Disclosures for yourself. To download, search on any search engine for "FTC .com Disclosures 2013" or visit https://s3.amazonaws.com/7mistakes/dotcomdisclosures.pdf.

Conclusion

The rules for online advertising are very complex.

For this reason, a good way to start with compliance is to ensure that you have a clear understanding of —

- puffery and how puffery is different from an ad claim, and

- the fact that ad claims are not just on your sales page; they may be other website pages, social media pages, blogs, videos.

Then you can stay clearly on the side of puffery until you determine that you need to cross the line to making an ad claim. At that time, you can review the substantiation rules and proceed with the ad claim and substantiation.

The worst of all situations would be to unintentionally make ad claims. Because if you make ad claims unintentionally, you certainly wouldn't be substantiating them.

Regarding how to make the required disclosures, It's important to note that the .com Disclosures are not definitive law, meaning that they are guidelines. So, compliance is voluntary; however, if you engage in practices contrary to the .com Disclosures, particularly if consumers have sent complaints to the FTC or if there is a pattern of noncompliance, you may very well get the dreaded knock on your door from the FTC.

7 Tragic (Legal) Mistakes That Can Get Your Bank Accounts Frozen By The FTC Leaving You Penniless...

Probably the most informative aspect of the .com Disclosures are the 22 examples provided in the Appendix of how to make the required disclosures. Download the .com Disclosures and carefully study and follow the examples. Search online for ".com Disclosures 2013" or visit https://s3.amazonaws.com/7mistakes/dotcomdisclosures.pdf.

Tragic Mistake 2

Failure To Follow the FTC Disclosure Rules For Testimonials

FTC Guides For Testimonials And Endorsements (2009)

On October 5, 2009, the FTC issued its revised Guides for the Use of Endorsements and Testimonials in advertising. The revised Guides focus on rules clarifying the use of endorsements in online advertising.

The Guides specify rules for marketers on the Internet, and they apply to two categories of marketers (these are the terms used by the FTC):

- *"advertisers"* – online marketers that recruit affiliates, resellers, and bloggers to promote the advertiser-suppliers' products and services, and

- *"endorsers"* – affiliates, resellers, and bloggers that promote products and services for advertiser-suppliers.

Since the term "advertiser" alone is not a very descriptive term, this discussion will utilize the term "advertiser-supplier" to indicate that advertiser-suppliers are marketers who *supply* products or services.

In a nutshell, the Guides are aimed at protection of online consumers. The FTC wants to regulate online marketers to see if they're trading testimonials and favorable reviews for some kind of financial reward or other benefit.

The Guides clearly establish the principle that both advertiser-suppliers and their endorsers may be held *liable* for unsubstantiated, false, and deceptive marketing statements.

Advertiser-Suppliers: When Do The FTC Disclosure Rules Apply?

The threshold question for online marketers is "when do the FTC disclosure rules apply to my marketing practices"?

If all you do is market directly from your website with no involvement by intermediaries such as affiliates, resellers, or bloggers, the FTC disclosure rules do not apply.

However, if you recruit intermediaries - such as affiliates, resellers, or bloggers - to pitch your products or services, and this even includes people whom you compensate or provide free promotional materials or benefits for writing testimonials that you post on your site, then the FTC disclosure rules apply, and you'd be classified as an advertiser-supplier.

Intermediaries would also include viral marketing programs with incentives and network marketing programs where endorsers periodically review your products or services, and they receive a free product or service about which they write a review. If you utilize these viral and network marketing programs, you'll also be classified as an advertiser-supplier.

If the FTC disclosure rules do apply, you may be held liable for the actions of your endorser.

This is the way the FTC put it:

"It is foreseeable that an endorser may exaggerate the benefits of a free product or fail to disclose a material relationship where one exists. In employing this means of marketing, the advertiser-supplier has assumed the risk that an endorser may fail to disclose a material connection or misrepresent a product, and the potential liability that accompanies that risk" (emphasis supplied).

If you're an advertiser-supplier, this potential liability should be a wake-up call.

Endorsers: When Do Disclosure Rules Apply?

Again, the threshold question "when do the FTC disclosure rules apply to me"?

7 Tragic (Legal) Mistakes That Can Get Your Bank Accounts Frozen By The FTC Leaving You Penniless...

If all you do on your website is publish creative content about your areas of interest or your own products or services, you're not regulated by the FTC disclosure rules.

However, if you're an intermediary (such as an affiliate, reseller, or blogger) for another online marketer, and you pitch someone else's products or services, in exchange for payment of money, you're clearly an endorser.

When you normally think of an endorser, you probably think of a celebrity or some other form of endorser, such as the pitch person on late night infomercials.

However, we all act as spokespersons frequently. We talk to our friends, and we post comments on social media, and in many cases these communications are acting as recommending a product or service. As such, we're also spokespersons.

Organizations can also take the role of a spokesperson. Corporations, colleges and universities, and professional organizations all share information about products or services, and in such cases they are acting as spokespersons.

There's a grey area in situations where you're not paid money, but you may receive some sort of benefit. Under certain circumstances, where the applicable facts indicate "sponsorship", you'll be regulated as an endorser.

The FTC disclosure rules drill down into this grey area by providing 3 scenarios where a consumer reviews a product or service:

7 Tragic Legal Mistakes That Can Get Your Bank Accounts Frozen By The FTC Leaving You Penniless...

- no endorsement - a consumer purchases a product with his/her own money, and posts a review or opinion on a blog (result: FTC disclosure rules do not apply because there is no relationship at all with the advertiser-supplier; no worries);

- no endorsement - same scenario, except that a coupon for a free trial of the product is generated by the store's computer, based on his/her purchases (result: FTC disclosure rules do not apply because there is no relationship with the advertiser-supplier indicating "sponsorship"; no worries); and

- endorsement - the consumer is part of a network marketing program where he/she periodically reviews products and receives a free product for which he/she writes reviews (result: FTC disclosure rules do apply because there is a relationship with the advertiser-supplier based on the stream of free products indicating "sponsorship"; there are legitimate worries about how to comply with the FTC disclosure rules).

A good example would be a dentist who recommends a particular brand of toothpaste and provides a complimentary sample for you. If the toothpaste manufacturer or its representative provided the samples to the dentist for free, this would put the dentist in the category of an endorser who has received a benefit.

How do you determine whether a statement is a testimonial? According to the FTC, the determination must be made solely from the perspective of the consumer. If the consumer would view the statement as influenced by the advertiser-supplier, it's covered by the FTC disclosure rules.

> **Tip:** You should always look at the question of whether to disclose through the eyes of the consumer. If the consumer might be influenced by a relationship, then it's material and it should be disclosed.

What Do The FTC Disclosure Rules Require Advertiser-Suppliers And Endorsers To Do?

If you're an *advertiser-supplier* that sponsors endorsers, the FTC disclosure rules require you to:

- provide guidance and training to your endorsers to help them understand their legal obligations regarding advertising statements about your products or services; primarily, that their claims are truthful, not misleading, and substantiated, and

- monitor your endorsers and take steps to remedy advertising statements, practices, or procedures that are unlawful. In essence, advertiser-suppliers should implement policies and procedures to ensure that their endorsers comply with the FTC disclosure rules.

- Also, you should disclose "material connections" you have with persons who provide endorsements and testimonials for you. "Material connections" involve the payment of money or providing free

7 Tragic Legal Mistakes That Can Get Your Bank Accounts Frozen By The FTC Leaving You Penniless...

promotional materials or benefits for the endorsements or testimonials.

- If you make a statement that refers to findings by a research organization, any "material connection" with the research organization must be disclosed.

- Remember that testimonials are considered to be ad claims, so the rules discussed in Tragic Mistake 1 apply. Level of success was significantly greater than typical, provided that a "results not typical" disclaimer accompanied the endorsement. Beginning in December, 2009, the "results not typical" disclaimer won't be effective any more. Now, you need a statement regarding the generally expected results.

If you're an *endorser* that is sponsored by an advertiser-supplier, the FTC disclosure rules require you to:

- disclose "material connections" involving the receipt of money or free promotional materials or benefits for promoting your advertiser-suppliers' products or services,

- if you *write a*n endorsement for a product or service, you must be a bona fide user who is writing based on actual experience at the time the endorsement is given (for example, writing a review of a book you haven't read or a product that you haven't tried out is a no-no), and

- disclose typical results that should reasonably be expected from a product or service ("results not typical" disclaimers won't work anymore).

What Do Endorsers Have To Say To Comply?

There are no precise rules. The best recommendation is to use common sense, and to clearly and succinctly disclose the relationship and benefit.

Basically, disclose if you got a complimentary product, or that you are an affiliate who may be paid a commission. For example –

- "Apple gave me this new iPad to try out."

- "I received a complimentary flight by Delta Air Lines."

Another example: for a paid celebrity endorser, a photo of the celebrity with the caption "Compensated Endorser".

You could even create a simple icon with the caption: "Disclosure – I get free stuff to review on my blog."

Use your imagination, be clever. But get the idea across that you're receiving compensation or other benefit.

The Reverb Communications Case: If You're Tempted To Use Fake Endorsements, Don't Do It!

The FTC's first case enforcing the FTC disclosure rules was against Reverb Communications which was settled in 2010.

At that time, Reverb Communications was a public relations firm representing major clients in the video game industry, including clients such as MTV Games and Harmonix, as well as smaller firms that sell mobile game apps via the iTunes store. According to the FTC, Reverb's fee often includes a percentage of the sale of its clients' gaming apps.

The iTunes store provides users the ability to post reviews of gaming applications that are available for purchase. These reviews include a rating system (based on a possible rating of one to five stars) and written text.

According to the FTC, during a period of approximately one year Reverb employees posted reviews in the iTunes store favorable to games of Reverb's clients. The reviews were posted in a manner that would convey the impression that disinterested consumers had posted them.

In addition to giving five-star ratings to Reverb's clients' games, Reverb's employees posted written endorsements such as:

- "Amazing new game",
- "ONE of the BEST", and
- "Really cool game".

The FTC brought suit claiming that Reverb Communications engaged in deceptive advertising by having its employees pose as ordinary consumers posting reviews, while failing to disclose that the reviews were from paid employees working on behalf of their clients. Reverb agreed to settle the case.

The basic lesson of the Reverb Communications case is clear – don't use employees or contractors to post fake endorsements under any circumstances.

The FTC stated in its press release announcing the Reverb Communications settlement: "Companies, including public relations firms involved in online marketing need to abide by long-held principles of truth in advertising. Advertisers should not pass themselves off as ordinary consumers touting a product...".

The FTC settlement with Reverb requires Reverb to remove the previously posted deceptive endorsements and to refrain from using employees to post fake reviews for its clients in the future.

Conclusion

The disclosure rules appear to be complex.

However, they're not as complex as they may seem if you –

- have a clear understanding of the difference between an advertiser-supplier and an endorser;

- have a clear understanding of the role you are playing in a given situation (you may be an advertiser-supplier in some situations and an endorser in others); and

- develop a few simple ways to make the required disclosures.

A basic understanding and awareness is really the key.

You can always look of the rules and guidelines as you develop your approach to compliance.

Tragic Mistake 3

You Offer A Biz Op Without Compliance With FTC Regulations

(Biz Ops Are A Trap For The Unwary Under The New Biz Op Rule!)

Effective on March 1, 2012, the FTC's new Business Opportunity Rule (New Biz Op Rule) became effective.

The Biz Op Rule applies to a specific type of offer defined as a "Business Opportunity" (Biz Op).

The FTC's objective with the New Biz Op rule was to make it tough to make legally compliant Biz Op offers, particularly Biz Op offers that make earnings claims.

The New Biz Op Rule

The New Biz Op Rule reduces a business opportunity seller's disclosure requirements with a new, streamlined page requiring 5 items of information.

However, the New Biz Op Rule expands the types of companies that are covered.

The New Biz Op Rule continues to apply to vending machines, rack displays, payphones, and Internet kiosks. However, the definition of a biz op now extends to work-at-home schemes such a jewelry assembly and envelope stuffing.

The New Biz Op Rule exempts franchisors covered by the FTC Franchise Rule and multi-level marketing companies.

Biz Op Defined

The New Biz Op Rule stipulates three elements that must be satisfied for an offer to be a Biz OP.

- Solicitation For New Business Opportunity - a seller solicits a prospective purchaser to enter into a "new business" (i.e. a new line or type of business that the prospect is not currently engaged in);

- "Required Payment" By Prospect – the prospect makes a payment, meaning all consideration paid by the prospect to the seller or an affiliate for the right to obtain or commence the operation of the business opportunity;

- Business Assistance – the seller (or someone recommended by the seller) provides any of the following types of assistance:

- Locations for the use or operation of equipment or other devices paid for by the prospect;
- Outlets, accounts, or customers; or
- Buy back promises for goods or services provided by the prospect.

Because the New Biz Op Rule imposes numerous detailed requirements, it's recommended that Internet marketers and online entrepreneurs should *not* offer Biz Ops, unless with close guidance and consultation from an attorney specializing in Biz Ops.

Even with careful attention to all the requirements, it would still be relatively easy to inadvertently cross the line into non-compliance, and therefor huge exposure to liability.

In a nutshell, offering Biz Ops is a high risk activity unless you intend to have access to expert legal guidance.

Tip: Absolutely the worst situation of all would be to inadvertently cross the line into Biz Op regulation without intending to be regulated as a Biz Op. That's why the following discussion will focus on how to *avoid* Biz Op regulation.

How To Avoid Biz Op Regulation

The way to avoid regulation as a Biz Op is to not satisfy one of the three elements of a Biz Op under the New Biz Op Rule. Remember, all three elements must be satisfied for a Biz Op to exist, so if you satisfy any two elements, but not three, you've avoided Biz Op regulation.

So, one way to avoid Biz Op regulation is to offer only educational and training services, and not offer a "new business". The FTC stated specifically that "general business advice and training" services are not included in the Biz OP definition. However, some of the typical offers by Internet marketers and online marketers may come close to crossing over from education and training to operation of a "new business".

However, if you analyze the three Biz Op elements, elements 1 and 2 may be satisfied by some offers typically made by Internet marketers and online entrepreneurs. With many offers there are "grey areas" with elements 1 and 2, where there's no way to determine with confidence whether you've satisfied the element or not.

- For example, the "new business" requirement of Element 1 does not mean a person who has never been in business. The "new business" could be satisfied by an offer to an experienced business person if the offer presents a new line of business to the prospect. Sellers generally have no way of knowing the present business status of prospects.

- Another example: The "required payment" requirement of Element 2 may be satisfied by indirect payments through a third party. Even if you split a product into a free part and paid part, you'll still satisfy the "required payment" requirement if the paid part is a "practical necessity" for obtaining or operating the business opportunity.

So, due to the relative uncertainty regarding elements 1 and 2, the recommended approach is to focus on not satisfying element 3, thereby avoiding Biz Op regulation.

Avoiding Element 3 – Business Assistance

Element 3 should be your primary focus in avoiding Biz Op regulation.

The key is to avoid providing business assistance by *not* offering to provide locations (this applies primarily to offline businesses), *outlets, accounts, customers*, or buy back promises.

This is how the FTC describes providing *outlets, accounts, or customers:*

"...requiring... recommending... [or] providing a list of... [or] collecting a fee on behalf of ... lead generating companies... or otherwise assisting the prospective purchaser in obtaining... outlets, accounts, or customers."

Remember that the FTC says that it's OK (meaning you *won't* be regulated as a Biz Op) if all you do is to provide "advertising and general advice about business development and training".

So, regarding Element 3, I'm often asked the following 2 questions by online marketers:

- Question 1: Is lead generation assistance to an Ecommerce website providing "Internet Customers" (which would also be regulated as a Biz OP)?

- Question 2: Does providing a turnkey ecommerce website amount to providing an "Internet Outlet (which would be regulated as a Biz OP)"?

The likely answer to Question 1 regarding lead generation is that you would probably be regulated as a Biz Op if your promises indicate that the purchaser has no risk in the transaction. In other words, if all the customer has to do is to purchase your lead generating opportunity, and you would find all the leads and customers (or be primarily involved in finding them), it certainly looks like a Biz Op. On the other hand, if all you provide is training, you should not be regulated as a Biz Op.

Regarding the answer to Question 2, the court in the 2014 case of the *FTC v. The Online Entrepreneur, Inc. (d/b/a The Six Figure Program), et. al.* reached a finding that surprised many online marketers (and a few attorneys, for that matter).

In the *Online Entrepreneur* case, the court held that the defendants' provision of turnkey websites for work–from–home customers constituted the sale of an "Internet outlet" that would trigger Biz Op regulation, despite the fact that training was offered. The result – the defendants were nailed for $2.9 Million for violation of Biz Op regulations and deceptive marketing practices.

This result in *Online Entrepreneur* was surprising to some, given past history to the effect that the sale of an old fashioned vending machine alone to a consumer was deemed not to be the sale of a Biz Op, unless the seller also promised to find outlets, accounts, or customers for the vending machine. So, if you analogize a vending machine to a turnkey website, it would seem the sale of the turnkey website alone would not trigger Biz Op regulation. Not so, according to the *Online Entrepreneur* decision!

One factor that may have been persuasive in *Online Entrepreneur* was the fact that the defendants were engaged in very aggressive earnings claims.

So, one significant question after the *Online Entrepreneur* decision is whether it's possible to sell turnkey websites to the work-from-home market without being regulated as a Biz Op. A close reading of the *Online Entrepreneur* decision seems to indicate a resounding "no"; it's not possible. We'll have to wait for future adjudicated cases to see if it's really possible, but for now, it's highly doubtful.

Tip: So, if you're selling turnkey websites to the work-from-market, you should strictly comply with Biz Op regulation, given the *Online Entrepreneur* decision. On the other hand, if you're selling turnkey websites to brick-and-mortar businesses, you should not be regulated by the Biz Op Rule.

Conclusion

The worst of all situations would be to unintentionally offer Biz Ops for sale. Because if you unintentionally offer Biz Ops, you certainly would not be in compliance with Biz Op regulation.

To avoid Biz Op regulation with confidence, understand the definition of Biz Op under the New Biz Op Rule, and be sure that you've *not* satisfied at least one of its three elements.

Offering Biz Ops is a high risk activity that should be avoided altogether, unless you have close guidance and consultation from an attorney specializing in Biz Ops.
.

Tragic Mistake 4

Failure To Provide The Required Disclosures For Your Membership Website

(Hint - Overlapping FTC & Little-Known State Regulations Now Make Continuity Programs The Most Regulated on the Web, and Penalties For Non-Compliance are Massive!)

> **Warning!** If you offer automatically renewed or continuous subscriptions for services in the United States, and specifically to California residents – including memberships, online or print content, or other subscription content – you're now among the most regulated businesses on the planet!

Continuity or Negative Option Plans

Plans that offer automatically renewed or continuous subscriptions for services have come under increased scrutiny and regulation from the U.S. Congress and the FTC. These plans are also described as:

- "continuity plans", or
- "negative option plans".

The key feature is that consumer charges are:

- automatically renewed, or
- continue periodically for an agreed upon time.

In a nutshell, the typical online businesses that are covered by these regulations are typically considered by Internet marketers and online entrepreneurs to be:

- membership sites, or
- subscription sites,
- this includes software-as-a-service (SaaS) sites as well.

ROSCA

In 2010, in reaction to numerous abuses by Internet scams involving continuity plans, the U.S. Congress passed the Restore Online Shopper's Confidence Act (ROSCA) which in part established three statutory rules for continuity programs:

- clearly and conspicuously disclose all material terms of the program prior to obtaining billing information (i.e. disclose the continuity program billing procedure prior to collecting credit card information), and

- obtain express informed consent before charging the consumer's account, and provide a simple mechanism for cancelling the plan.

The FTC was tasked with the responsibility of enforcement of ROSCA. Violations of ROSCA are treated as violations of FTC Act's prohibition of unfair or deceptive marketing acts or practices.

Nominal-Fee-To-Pay Offers

Since its enactment, the FTC has been active in enforcement of ROSCA. Two recent cases sent the message of aggressive FTC enforcement loud and clear: one for a settlement of $359 million and another was litigated for a verdict of $18 million.

Both of these cases involved what are generally known as "nominal-fee-to-pay offers", meaning that the consumer is lured into a continuity program with a an offer at a nominal charge (typically only a shipping and handling charge to get the customer's credit card information).

With a "nominal-fee-to-pay offer, the initial offer is:

- followed up with an upsell to a free trial, and

- when the free trial period expires, the consumer's card is then charged periodically until the consumer cancels.

> **Tip:** – One of the takeaways of these cases involving "nominal-fee-to-pay offers" is that the call to action for the nominal fee offer should have also provided the required ROSCA disclosures.

The FTC made it clear that even if the consumer is informed later (after the consumer accepts the nominal fee offer); it's a deceptive practice if you don't provide the ROSCA disclosures at the time of the call to action for the nominal fee offer.

California False Advertising Act – SB 340

The SB 340 amendments to the California False Advertising Act add these requirements for offers of automatically renewed or continuous subscriptions for services:

- a clear and conspicuous display of written terms (not a link) in visual proximity to the request for consent;

- an acknowledgement of renewal terms, cancellation policy, and how to cancel; and

- a clear and conspicuous notice of material changes and how to cancel.

Some of these requirements overlap with the ROSCA requirements, and some do not.

Compliance With Both ROSCA And SB 340

The real question is – how to comply both with ROSCA and SB 340 if you have a membership site, subscription site, or a SaaS site?

The following steps are recommended:

- Offer terms: the offer terms should be provided in written form (not a link), and should be separated by the size, type, or color of surrounding text; for visual proximity, place them above the call to action; all of the above should be prior to collecting billing information.

- Express, informed consent: after presentation of the offer terms, but before charging the customer's account, require the customer to click on an I AGREE button.

- Email acknowledgement: after the customer has given express, informed consent, email an acknowledgement of the consent to the customer; the acknowledgement email should provide the offer terms, cancellation policy, and information regarding how to cancel; recommend that the customer retain the email for future reference.

7 Tragic (Legal) Mistakes That Can Get Your Bank Accounts Frozen By The FTC Leaving You Penniless...

- Cancellation mechanism: customers should have a cancellation mechanism that is simple and easy to use.

- Notice of modifications: if there are changes to the terms of the offer, email the customer with a clear email heading providing easily understandable information in detail regarding the changes and how to cancel.

> **Note:** – If you offer a continuity plan – essentially, any plan for automatically renewed or continuous subscriptions for services to California residents – including memberships, online or print content, or other subscription content, you're now required to comply with two sets of regulations – one for ROSCA and another for the California False Advertising Act (SB 340).

Violations Can Result in Huge Fines

The consequences for violations of ROSCA and California SB 340 are huge:

- FTC sanctions for ROSCA violations of up to **$16,000 PER VIOLATION!**

- California sanctions of **$2,500 PER VIOLATION**!

Conclusion

Membership websites are attractive because they provide continuity income.

In response to numerous abuses by Internet scammers —

- the U.S. Congress passed the Restore Online Shopper's Confidence Act (ROSCA), and

- the State of California passed The SB 340 amendments to the California False Advertising Act.

Now, continuity plans are highly regulated, and the price for non-compliance is huge.

Internet marketers and online entrepreneurs will need to strictly comply with both laws in order to enjoy the benefits on continuity income going forward.

7 Tragic (Legal) Mistakes That Can Get Your Bank Accounts Frozen By The FTC Leaving You Penniless...

Tragic Mistake 5

Failure to Honor Your Privacy Policy & Make the Required Remarketing Disclosures

Part 1
Privacy Regulation Background And Fundamentals

Background

You're an online entrepreneur, or maybe you even view yourself as an "IM", and Internet marketer - a special breed of cat that's a subset of online entrepreneurs.

In either case, it doesn't matter if you're a veteran or a beginner. It doesn't even matter if you work in a home office, or in a real, brick and mortar office. You know one

important, overriding thing.

And that's the value of your email marketing list. The holy

grail of online marketing.

With a responsive email list, you can grow your business. You can market additional products, services, or information you might create in the future.

Or, you may market complimentary stuff of others – your JV partners.

You've known from day 1 that the single greatest asset of your growing online business is your email marketing list. That's why you expend so much time and effort growing it.

What you probably don't know is this – it's what I call the "great paradox". The fact that your most valuable asset is also your single greatest source of legal liability. Massive liability that could shut your business down in a single day.

This critical fact has been known by Internet attorneys like me for some time. But among online entrepreneurs and IM's, not very much at all.

And this is a huge problem if you continue to focus solely on building your list - at the expense of caring for it and protecting yourself as you grow and use it.

> **Tip:** – You absolutely, positively need to pay more attention to protecting your email list and yourself. And that begins with understanding what information is privacy-protected!

How Privacy Regulation Began in the United States

Certain information is privacy-protected. It's protected so much by the FTC that it's almost viewed as sacred. And this is the basis for all legal regulations that affect your list.

The best way to get a perspective on privacy-protected information is to understand how privacy regulation began in the United States.

It all started back in 2004 in California, not in the U.S. Congress. The California Online Privacy Protection Act (OPPA) became effective on July 1, 2004.

OPPA requires website operators who collect online "personally identifiable information" from California residents to post a Privacy Policy on their websites. So, at the time of the beginning of formal privacy protection in the U.S. privacy-protected information was limited to "personally identifiable information" which included:

- first name, last name,
- street address,
- email address,
- phone number, and
- social security number

In addition, privacy-protected information included other information if linked to any of the above elements of "personally identifiable information" such as:

- height
- weight

- occupation
- birth date
- etc.

After OPPA went into effect, websites selling the products into the United States began to post Privacy Policies that were OPPA-compliant. This was the result for two basic reasons:

- it would have been difficult to screen out California residents with confidence, and

- who among Internet marketers and online entrepreneurs would want to screen out California residents anyway, since California is such a large market.

So, in essence, OPPA became a *de facto* federal statute of general application, meaning that it applied the general market, and was not restricted in application to specific markets.

There are federal statutes that protect privacy of specific information (as distinguished from statutes of general application such as OPPA). A few of these are :

- Health Insurance Portability and Accountability Act of 1996 (HIPAA) for patient health records,

- Gramm-Leach-Bliley Act (GLBA) for financial information,

- Children's Online Privacy Protection Act (COPPA) for personal information of children under age 13, and,

- Fair Credit Reporting Act (FCRA) for data collected by consumer reporting agencies.

Note: To this day, however, California's OPPA statute is the only privacy statute of general application in the U.S. The FTC regulates privacy under the general principles of Section 5 of the FTC Act. For more information regarding the FTC's authority, see the Chapter titled "What Does This Mean to You".

Social Media-Related Additions To Privacy-Protected Information

One big headache for Internet marketers and online entrepreneurs is that privacy-protected information is a moving target, meaning that it changes from time to time, as new technology leads to new privacy concerns.

Warning! – Because privacy-protection information is in a constant state of evolution, marketers must remain vigilant for new additions, or risk huge fines for non-compliance with ever-expanding privacy regulations.

For example, perceived abuses regarding social media caused the FTC to expand the scope of privacy-protected information.

On March 20, 2011, the FTC announced its proposed settlement regarding Google's social media online service known as "BUZZ".

In the proposed settlement, the FTC added new categories of privacy-protected information, which include:

- Physical location data,
- screen names, and
- lists of contacts.

> **Tip:** Beginning with the Google settlement on March 20, 2011, marketers must treat physical location data, screen names, and lists of contacts as privacy-protected information.

Mobile App-Related Privacy Rules

Both the State of California and the FTC have moved to regulate the booming market for mobile phone applications known as "apps".

Privacy concerns were heightened as a result of several incidents involving mobile phones, including:

- a blogger discovered that a social network app had uploaded his mobile phone contacts without permission,

- a photo sharing app also was found to upload user's contact without permission, and

- Twitter acknowledged uploading users' contacts from mobile phones without permission.

On February 22, 2012, the California Attorney General announced that the California Online Privacy Protection Act (OPPA) applies not only to protected information collected through websites, but also via apps on mobile devices.

The result: mobile apps that collect privacy-protected information, including physical location data, from California residents should have a Privacy Policy just as websites do.

Shortly thereafter in August, 2012, the FTC jumped on the mobile app privacy bandwagon by announcing in its report titled "Marketing Your Mobile App – Get it Right From The Start" that, among other requirements, mobile app publishers should:

- get express, affirmative consent before collecting sensitive data such as "geo-location", medical, or financial data, and

- obtain verified parental consent before collecting personal information from children under 13 (U-13's).

> **Tip**: Social media and mobile apps are just the latest developments that trigger new privacy regulations. New regulations will be coming down the pike at an increasing rate. Keep up and comply with them, or suffer huge headaches and massive fines!

What to Do About Your Collection And Use of Protected Information

Once you know what information is privacy-protected, it's critical that you know what to do about it in terms of disclosures in your Privacy Policy.

In general terms, your Privacy Policy, regardless of whether it is posted on your website or via your mobile app, should disclose the following:

- the dates that the Privacy Policy takes effect,

- the categories of privacy-protection information collected,

- how privacy-protected information is collected,

- how users may change privacy-protected information,

- the process for notification regarding changes to the Privacy Policy, and

- how privacy-protected information is shared or made accessible to others, particularly for marketing purposes.

Part 2
Do What You Say And Don't Do What You Say You Won't To Avoid FTC Lawsuits For Deceptive Advertising

The FTC, in its August, 2012 report titled "Marketing Your Mobile App – Get it Right From The Start" put it this way regarding mobile apps, but it reflects the FTC's policy generally:

"Honor your privacy promises."

You're probably thinking: But we don't make any promises.' Think again and reread your privacy policy or what you say about your privacy settings. Chances are you make assurances to users about the security standards you apply or what you do with their personal information. At minimum, app developers – like all other marketers – have to live up to those promises. The FTC has taken action against dozens of companies that claimed to safeguard the privacy or security of users' information, but didn't live up to their promises in the day-to-day operation of their business. The FTC also has taken action against businesses that made broad statements about their privacy practices, but then failed to disclose the extent to which they collected or shared information with others – like advertisers or other app developers."

The FTC treats the statements in your Privacy Policy just as it would treat your ad claims for purposes of "deceptive" practices.

As discussed in the first chapter titled "The Internet Landscape Has Changed!" FTC says that an ad claim is deceptive if it:

- Is likely to mislead consumers acting reasonably under the circumstances; and

- Is "material" - that is, important to a consumer's decision to buy or use the product or service?

So, this logically leads to the Cardinal Rule that the FTC expects you to follow:

Cardinal Rule – Regarding your Privacy Policy, be sure to do what you say and don't do what you say you won't. If you violate this Cardinal Rule, you will be liable for an FTC claim for "deceptive" practices!

Examples of Cardinal Rule Claims Taken From Actual FTC Cases

- The FTC Settlement With Google – In 2011, the FTC settled claims with Google regarding alleged "deceptive" practices involving Google's BUZZ service. The FTC pointed to Google's Privacy Policy which stated: "When you sign up for a particular service that requires registration, we ask you to provide personal information. If we use this information in a manner different than the purpose for which it was collected, then we will ask for your consent prior to such use." The FTC *alleged* that Google violated this promise by shifting Gmail users to its new BUZZ service without permission.

- The FTC Settlement With Chitka – Also in 2011, the FTC settled claims with Chitka regarding alleged "deceptive practices" involving the passing of cookies to consumers. The FTC pointed to Chitka's Privacy Policy which promised that consumers could opt out of having cookies passed to their browsers. The FTC *alleged* that Chitka violated this promise when the opt out lasted only 10 days.

- The FTC Settlement With Twitter – In 2010, the FTC settled claims against Twitter involving data security lapses that permitted two hackers to access users accounts. The FTC pointed to Twitter's Privacy Policy which stated: "We employ administrative, physical, and electronic measures designed to protect your information from unauthorized access." The FTC alleged that Twitter violated this promise by using weak passwords that used lowercase, common dictionary words.

7 Tragic (Legal) Mistakes That Can Get Your Bank Accounts Frozen By The FTC Leaving You Penniless...

Don't Shoot Yourself in the Foot With Careless and Overbroad Statements

If you apply the rules regarding "deceptive" ad claims, you can see why certain statements you may make in your Privacy Policy and squeeze pages, may easily be construed as "deceptive", depending on how they are worded.

The result – you've unwittingly shot yourself in the foot!

For example, consider this classic statement: WE WILL NEVER SELL OR RENT YOUR PERSONAL INFORMATION. "Never" means exactly that – never!

Now think this through. Let's parse the statement. Isn't it likely that you may sell your online business or website in the future? And isn't it likely that you may share protected information with JV partners and resellers? If you do, you'd be in violation of your promise.

And wouldn't this promise be material to your list? Of course it would!

So, the promise with the term "never" is at least deceptive, and probably not true on its face. You should always be wary of absolute statements regarding use and sharing of protected information.

A better approach would be to change the statement to read (assuming its true) to:

- WE WILL NEVER SELL OR RENT YOUR PERSONAL INFORMATION FOR DIRECT MARKETING PURPOSES, or

- WE WILL NEVER SELL OR RENT YOUR PERSONAL INFORMATION WITHOUT YOUR PRIOR OPTIN CONSENT.

Tip: Avoid making absolute statements regarding your use and sharing of protected information.

Tip: If possible, qualify your statements regarding your use and sharing of protected information so that they are not absolute.

Another area where it's easy to make a statement that's deceptive is with outlandish claims for data security.

For example, WE PROTECT YOUR INFORMATION WITH THE HIGHEST INDUSTRY STANDARDS FOR DATA SECURITY.

Again, let's parse the statement. What are the HIGHEST industry standards for data security? Does HIGHEST mean military grade security? Does it mean compliance with ISO standards?

You may always deliver extremely high levels of data security; however, you're way better off to promise no more than what the FTC requires - WE WILL PROVIDE REASONABLE AND ADEQUATE SECURITY.

> **Tip**: Boilerplate Privacy Policies usually don't protect you because they make "standard" privacy statements that may not apply to you, and in many cases they fail to make statements that you should make regarding your actual marketing practices involving the collection, use, and sharing of privacy-protected information. For this reason, it's always recommended that you have a Privacy Policy that's tailored to your specific marketing practices.

Part 3
Provide The Required Disclosures For Your Remarketing Practices To Avoid FTC Lawsuits and Being Banned From The Major Platforms Such As Google And Facebook

What Are Remarketing Ads?

Generally speaking, there are 2 types of online ads –

- Contextual ads – based on the context of the website, and

- Remarketing ads through behavioral targeting (interest-based ads).

This is how contextual ads and remarketing ads would differ based on an example of a website based on the salt water fishing niche –

- Contextual ads - ads related to salt water fishing only (i.e. rods and reels), and

- Remarketing ads – on the same salt water fishing website, ads for men's formal wear (or anything else) based on the visitor's past browsing history of websites dedicated to men's formal wear.

Remarketing ads have also been described by marketers as "behavioral ads, "targeted ads, and "interest-based ads."

The key to remarketing ads is that they are based on a user's demonstrated interests based on past websites visited, articles read, products purchased, etc.

From an online marketer's perspective, the good thing about remarketing ads is that they convert to sales at a significantly higher rate than contextual ads.

From the user's perspective, the good thing about remarketing ads is that user sees only ads that the user is interested in. On the other hand, many users view remarketing ads as a serious invasion of privacy.

> **Tip:** If you haven't yet experimented with remarketing ads, you should give it a try because the conversion rates are significantly improved over contextual ad conversions. However, if you do, you need to be very careful to periodically review your Privacy Policy to ensure compliance with FTC requirements as well as the terms of use for the remarketing platforms you use such as Google and Facebook.

The FTC Gets Involved With Remarketing Ads

Guess what? When consumers view an advertising practice as an invasion of privacy, the FTC gets involved!

On February 12, 2009, the FTC issued its *Self-Regulatory Principles for Online Behavioral Advertising* for purposes of establishing its principles for online behavioral ads.

The key word in the title to the FTC's document is "Self-Regulatory", meaning that the FTC expects the Internet industry to self-regulate (i.e. manage itself without specific regulations).

- But don't be fooled into thinking that the Self-Regulatory Principles are voluntary – they're not!

- Just look at what one of the FTC Commissioners said regarding a report issued in 2012 by the FTC regarding "recommendations" for consumer privacy to the effect that it would be a mistake to assume that the report's recommendations are "voluntary", stating that Internet marketers that do not comply with the report's "best practices" may "face the wrath of the [FTC]".

And industry leaders in the field of remarketing ads such as Google and Facebook have definitely not regarded the Self-Regulatory Principles as voluntary.

- These industry leaders have integrated the Self-Regulatory Principles into their terms of service.

- And failure to comply can get you *banned from participation*!

This is how the FTC defines remarketing ads -

- Tracking of a consumer's online activities,

- Over time (including searches conducted, web pages visited, content viewed),

- To deliver ads targeted to the individual consumer's interests.

The FTC refers to Remarketing Ads as "online behavioral ads" or "OBA".

It's important to understand that, according to the FTC, OBA does not include –

- First party ads (no data is shared with 3rd parties), and

- Contextual ads.

The FTC's 4 Self-Regulatory Principles for disclosures regarding OBA are listed below. These disclosures are typically made in a Privacy Policy.

Principle 1 – Transparency and Consumer Control:

- Clear, concise, consumer-friendly, and prominent statement,

- Data is being collected for OBA,

- Consumers can choose whether or not to have their information collected, and

- Clear, easy-to-use, and accessible method of opting out.

Principle 2 – Reasonable Security, and Limited Data Retention, for Consumer Data:

- Provide reasonable security, and

- Retain data only as long as necessary to fulfill a legitimate business or law enforcement need.

Principle 3 – Affirmative Express Consent for Material Changes to Existing Privacy Promises:

- Privacy Policy changes that are materially different from prior promises are not retroactive, and

- Affirmative express consent is required for affected consumers.

Principle 4 – Affirmative Express Consent to (or Prohibition Against) Using Sensitive Data for OBA:

- Health data,
- Location (GPS) data,
- Financial data, and
- Social Security Numbers.

Google And Facebook Respond To The FTC's Self-Regulatory Principles

Google and Facebook have responded to the FTC's self-regulatory principles by integration of the principles into their terms of service and by *banning violators from participation in their remarketing programs!*

Google's Disclosure Requirements

Google's Adwords Requirements –

- Description of how you're using remarketing,
- Description of how 3rd party vendors such as Google use OBA across the Web,

- Description of how 3rd party vendors such as Google use cookies based on past visits to a website, and

- Information about how to optout.

Google Analytics For Display Advertising Requirements (Remarketing with Google Analytics, Google Display Network Impression Reporting, the DoubleClick Campaign Manager integration, and Google Analytics Demographics and Interest Reporting) -

- Description of the advertising features implemented,

- Describe how you and 3rd party vendors use 1st party cookies (such as the Google Analytics cookie) and 3rd party cookies (such as the DoubleClick cookie) or other 3rd party identifiers together,

- Describe how visitor can optout, and

- Provide information regarding DoubleClick advertising cookies.

Facebook's Disclosure Requirements

Facebook's Custom Audience enables a website to display OBA to website's list members when they visit Facebook.com –

- Provide appropriate notice and consent,

- Provide optout mechanism (not directly required, but indirectly required), and

- Honor optouts - do not include persons who opted out.

State of California's Disclosure Requirements

Even the State of California is involved in OBA. California requires disclose in your Privacy Policy:

- That you to disclose how your website responds to "do-not-track" signals,

- Your response only requires disclosure of how you respond, if at all (there's no requirement that you honor "do-not-track" signals), and

- Fines for violators are up to $2,500 per violation.

Conclusion

Many Internet marketers and online entrepreneurs believe that privacy regulation does not directly affect them.

Nothing could be farther from the truth because privacy regulation directly affects the value of your email marketing list - the holy grail of online marketing.

It's critically important to understand that your Privacy Policy must reflect what you actually do in terms of collection, use, and sharing of the personal information you have in your marketing list.

For this reason, it's important to review and to update your Privacy Policies periodically – to ensure they are current and consistent to your marketing practices.

Never lose sight of the fact that one of the most important keys for privacy compliance is to always honor the promises you make in your Privacy Policy – do what you say you'll do, and don't do the things you say you won't!

Remarketing also known as "Online behavioral Advertising" (OBA) is increasing in momentum on the Web. The associated increase in conversion rates is well established, and major players such as Google and Facebook continue to refine their OBA programs.

Given the privacy concerns among some consumers, the FTC continues to closely monitor OBA developments and use.

For now, the FTC has chosen to remain on the sidelines by simply issuing guidelines for self regulation from the online industry.

Don't be fooled into believing the FTC's OBA guidelines are voluntary. Google and Facebook certainly don't.

Your Privacy Policy is your vehicle for the required behavioral ad and OBA disclosures, and if you engage in behavioral advertising and OBA, failure to make and to maintain these disclosures, can not only get you sued by the

FTC for deceptive marketing practices, but also banned by major OBA platforms such as Google and Facebook.

Tip: Great benefits await online marketers who use behavioral ads and OBA, but great care must be taken with periodic Privacy Policy reviews to ensure Privacy Policy disclosure compliance in order to avoid legal liability and loss of rights to participate on major platforms.

Tragic Mistake 6

Failure to Manage Rogue Affiliates Who Get You Sued For Their Deceptive Marketing Practices

(Because You Didn't Manage Them!)

Internet marketers and online entrepreneurs often ask: Am I liable if any of my affiliates engage in deceptive marketing practices?

The answer is, it depends on specific facts and circumstances, but it all comes down to management of affiliates.

We only have to look to recent FTC cases to learn that affiliate marketers have been nailed for engaging in deceptive marketing practices involving –

- false and unsubstantiated claims,

- false news reports,

- untrue claims of test results, and

- testimonials that were completely fabricated.

- And in one recent case, an Internet marketer with ineffective FTC legal forms was held liable for failing to monitor affiliates' marketing practices.

Internet marketers and online entrepreneurs should understand that the legal violations of affiliates may result in liability for the Internet marketer, particularly where an Internet marketer fails to monitor and terminate affiliates who engage in deceptive marketing practices.

For this reason, it's absolutely critical that Internet marketers and online entrepreneurs who use affiliates understand how to avoid this liability.

Basic Truth In Advertising Principles

These principles are discussed in more detail in Tragic Mistake 1, but a summary follows.

- Claims by marketers regarding a product or service that would materially influence a consumer's decision must be truthful, not misleading, and reasonably substantiated prior to publication.

  o Being truthful is a no-brainer. However, if the claim is technically true, but it omits a material factor that a consumer would consider, then it would also be deceptive.

- o And claims about objective, specific results must be substantiated by tests prior to publication or else they're also deceptive.

- Ditto for claims made endorsers and testimonialists about someone else's product or service. The same rules summarized above also apply to endorsers and testimonialists who make claims or statements about the products of others.

- If a marketer doesn't have proof that an endorser's "success story" experience represents what consumers will achieve by using the product, the advertising copy must clearly and conspicuously disclose the generally expected results in the depicted circumstances.

  - o Prior to December, 2009, it was OK to use an endorser's "success story" endorsement, even if the endorser's level of success was significantly greater than typical, provided that a "results not typical" disclaimer accompanied the endorsement.

  - o Beginning in December, 2009, the "results not typical" disclaimer will no longer be effective.

  - o Now, a statement regarding the generally expected results is required.

- If there's a "material relationship" (family or employment relationship or payment or benefits) between the marketer and an endorser or testimonialist that would affect how people evaluate the endorsement or testimonial, it should be disclosed "clearly and conspicuously".

The Problem With Affiliate Marketers

Affiliate marketers are engaged in performance marketing, meaning –

- that they are compensated on a "performance" basis involving a completed action.

- In most situations, affiliates are compensated based on conversions originated through traffic driven to the advertiser's website.

The problem with affiliates in terms of marketing practices is that –

- performance-based compensation for affiliates creates an inverse relationship between maximizing conversions on the one hand, and

- on the other hand providing marketing messages that comply with the truth in advertising rules discussed above.

Tip: The FTC is very concerned about rogue affiliates who take deceptive marketing practices to a whole new level. If there was any question about it, I got the message loud and clear from a top FTC official at a technology law conference. Expect new developments in this area.

What is Required If You Market Through Affiliate Networks

The FTC requires that Internet marketers have reasonable programs in place to train and monitor their affiliates.

The key question is what is "reasonable" according to the FTC?

The FTC says that what is reasonable varies with the circumstances.

- According to the FTC, if the product or service at issue could cause consumer harm – either physical injury or financial loss – then a relatively high level of supervision would be required.

- For example, health products may require more supervision than the promotion of ladies hand bags.

Core elements of an affiliate monitoring program should always include:

- Consistent with an Internet marketer's responsibility for substantiating objective product claims, Internet marketers should explain to affiliates the marketing message regarding the product or service, including what can be said and what can't be said about the product or service.

- These explanations should be consistent with the basic truth in advertising principles discussed above.

- Set up and maintain a reasonable monitoring program to determine what affiliates are actually saying about the product or service.

- Follow up with questionable affiliate marketing practices, and terminate affiliates who willfully or repeatedly do not follow the rules.

A recent settlement with an Internet marketer imposed more stringent requirements.

- Clearly and conspicuously disclose in writing to each marketing affiliate that engaging in deceptive marketing practices will result in immediate termination of the affiliate relationship and forfeiture of all monies owed to such marketing affiliate.

- Routinely monitor and review, on at least a monthly basis at times not disclosed in advance to the affiliate and in a manner reasonably calculated not to disclose the monitoring activity at the time it is conducted, affiliate marketing materials, including websites, emails, banners, sponsored search terms, and pop-up ads.

- Promptly and completely investigate any consumer complaint regarding any affiliate.

- Immediately halt the processing of any payments or charges generated by an affiliate that the Internet marketer knows or should know is engaged in a deceptive marketing practice.

- Fully refund, within five business days, each consumer charged by any defendant whose sale originated from any affiliate engaging in a deceptive marketing practice.

- Terminate immediately any affiliate that is engaged in deceptive marketing practices.

Conclusion

Internet marketers and online entrepreneurs who do not monitor and manage their marketing affiliates regarding deceptive marketing practices do so at their peril.

Both the FTC and state regulatory authorities are becoming increasingly more vigilant regarding online advertising and marketing, particularly regarding affiliate marketers.

At the very least, Internet marketers and online entrepreneurs should implement programs consistent with the core elements discussed above.

It remains to be seen whether the more stringent requirements implemented in the recent FTC settlement with an Internet marketer who was actively engaged in deceptive marketing practices himself will also apply to Internet marketers who have no past record of deceptive practices.

7 Tragic (Legal) Mistakes That Can Get Your Bank Accounts Frozen By The FTC Leaving You Penniless...

Tragic Mistake 7

Your Social Media Giveaways Get You Sued For Running an Illegal Lottery

(And All You Wanted To Do Was To Have A Simple Giveaway Contest On Facebook! Go Figure!)

Why Social Media Promotions Are Important

Social media promotions - giveaways, sweepstakes, and contests - are important whether you're a big business (pick one), a national franchise chain (say, McDonalds), or a small ecommerce business (you) because they, if used creatively and skillfully –

- grow social influence,

- improve organic search rankings,

- increase Web traffic,

- increase brand awareness,

- attract qualified prospects, and
- increase conversions.

In short, they are great marketing tools.

The problem is that giveaways have been abused in the past by unscrupulous marketers.

Back in the day, it was common to require a person to make a purchase to enter a giveaway contest. The problem was that purchased item never came or it was junk. There were other abuses as well.

So, Is It Really True That Giving Stuff Away For Free Is Legally Regulated?

The short answer is, yes.

Now giveaways are highly regulated. And if you sponsor or host one – even a simple one on Facebook – without complying with the various federal and state laws, you can get you into big trouble.

The problem for most Internet marketers and online entrepreneurs is that sponsorship and hosting of social media promotions is often overlooked and completely misunderstood.

The result is that most Internet marketers and online entrepreneurs who sponsor and host social media promotions do so at significant legal risk.

The discussion in this chapter is intended to explain how to enjoy the benefits of social media promotions while managing legal risk and exposure.

The 3 Types of Giveaways Or Promotions

All giveaways – regardless of their names or what they're called – will fall into 1 of these 3 categories .

- Sweepstakes – prize giveaways where winners are chosen by *chance*, essentially by luck of the draw.

- Contests – prizes for winners are chosen by *skill or merit*, such as best article, best video, best marketing strategy –

    o by qualified judges,

    o who evaluate contestants and choose winners based on objective criteria.

- Lotteries – random drawings for prizes where participants *pay to play*; lotteries have 3 elements –

    o prize,

    o chance, and

    o consideration (discussed below).

Lotteries are highly regulated by various states (they're considered to be gambling), and the costs for sponsoring or hosting a lottery are generally considerably beyond the resources of small, online businesses. In any event, lotteries require close legal supervision to avoid liability.

How To Avoid Lottery Regulation?

The primary concern of any Internet marketer or online entrepreneur who wants to sponsor or host a giveaway, should be to ensure that the giveaway is *not* a regulated lottery.

> **Tip:** Above all else, avoid regulation as a lottery! A lottery is gambling, and all states jealously protect against illegal lotteries. After all, many states operate lotteries, and they don't like the competition.

To avoid being liable for operating an illegal lottery, one of the 3 elements of a lottery – prize, chance, consideration - needs to fail.

- Prize – a giveaway needs a prize, so this element is not a failure candidate. You can't get around this one.

- Chance – if you want to run a *contest* (not a sweepstakes) you could get around chance – luck of the draw – by adding a requirement that involves voting or skill if you want to run a contest, but you couldn't have chance involved if you want to run a sweepstakes.

- Consideration – if you want to run a *sweepstakes*, (not a contest) avoid the requirement of entrants giving something of value, then you could avoid lottery regulation

---

Tip: All you have to do to avoid promoting an illegal lottery is to avoid one of the 3 elements above. The easiest element to avoid is *chance*, and for this reason, most of your giveaways will be Sweepstakes.

Running A Sweepstakes – Avoiding Consideration

The problem with hanging your hat on avoiding the *consideration* element to run a sweepstakes is that what constitutes consideration is not always clear.

For example, if an entrant is required to pay money to play, such as with state-run lotteries, then it's clear that the payment of money to play is consideration.

But there are other forms of consideration that are not obvious which could satisfy the consideration element making you liable for running an illegal lottery, and you don't even know it. And to complicate matters, different states have different approaches to what qualifies as consideration.

That's because consideration involves giving something of value. So, what kind of value equals consideration?

- Requiring some to "like" you on Facebook or to "+1" you on Google+ could be considered consideration.

- Requiring the posting of a comment, sending multiple re-tweets, sharing a post on Google+, referring a friend, or completing a survey could definitely be considered consideration.

So, the big question is how to eliminate any doubt regarding avoiding the consideration element in running a sweepstakes?

The answer is to offer a completely free alternate means to enter the sweepstakes (i.e. without "liking", "+1"ing, or any other form of response). Alternate means to enter could include entry by mail or an online entry form (used most often).

Alternate forms of entry should be presented with equal prominence as the presentation for the entrants who actually provide the "liking", "+1"ing, or any other form of response.

Sweepstakes Rules

Official rules are required for all sweepstakes by the laws of all 50 states. Care must be taken at the outset with the official rules because they are not subject to change during the term of the sweepstakes.

Official rules for state laws must cover the following –

- The alternative form of entry that has an equal chance as other entrants by other methods;

- "No purchase necessary" statements made clearly and conspicuously;

- "Void where prohibited" statement;
- Beginning and end dates for the contest;
- Eligibility requirements;
- Description of prizes, including number of prizes, approximate retail value, and odds of winning each prize;
- How and when prizes will awarded and notification of winners;
- Where and when a list of winners can be obtained; and
- Complete name and contact information for sponsor of the contest.

How Does The FTC Get Involved In Sweepstakes?

The FTC gets involved (together with the various state attorneys general) with the *presentation* of the official rules.

The concern is that the official rules be presented fairly and conspicuously and not obscured with fine print or back door entry.

7 Tragic (Legal) Mistakes That Can Get Your Bank Accounts Frozen By The FTC Leaving You Penniless...

Tip: to pass muster with the FTC for presentation -
- include an abbreviated version of the official rules close to the entry form, and
- add a click-through mechanism acknowledging the opportunity to review the official rules.

Running A Contest – Avoiding Chance

Remember, to avoid running an illegal lottery with a contest, the *chance* element needs to be eliminated and substituted with skill or merit.

Just as with sweepstakes, contests are regulated by state laws.

To complicate matters several states do not allow purchase requirements (i.e. consideration) even for contests, such as Colorado, Maryland, Nebraska, North Dakota, and Vermont. So, legal review is necessary to ensure that entrants from all states that do not allow purchase requirement are excluded from the contest.

Official rules for contests include –

- The cost to enter, including all levels of the contest;

- How to participate in the contest, including all levels of the contest;

- A description and identity of the judges, criteria and weight for judging, and method of judging;

- Description of prizes, including number of prizes, approximate retail value;

- How and when prizes will awarded and notification of winners;

- The geographic area of the contest;

- Beginning and end dates for the contest;

- Where and when a list of winners can be obtained; and

- Complete name and contact information for sponsor of the contest.

Tip: to pass muster with the elimination of chance –

- Winners should be chosen only by established and conspicuously disclosed skill criteria;

- To resolve ties for the winner, there should be either an additional contest based entirely on skill, or award equal prizes to the ties. Do not draw names "from the hat" because that introduces chance to the determination of the winner.

Conclusion

The sponsorship and hosting of social media promotions is often overlooked and completely misunderstood.

To avoid significant legal risks and liability exposure with sponsoring and hosting social media promotions, it is critical to avoid running an illegal lottery.

Of the two other types of social media giveaways – sweepstakes and contests – running sweepstakes is generally preferred due to the fact that several states do not allow purchase requirements for contests.

What Are Your Options For A Real Legal Solution You Can Actually Have Confidence In?

Option 1: Hire an Internet Attorney

Your first option, and it's the best option, is to hire an experienced Internet attorney. It's always recommended that you hire an Internet attorney.

But there are also questions with this option:

- How to source, how to find an Internet attorney you can trust and have confidence in. The best source is to get a referral from someone you trust. The next best source is the martindale.com website. And be sure to look for the AV rating, it's the highest rating they give.

- There are also questions about turnaround time – sometimes working with a busy attorney doesn't quite fit your tight schedule when you're trying to get a new site online fast.

- However, the big question, and I talk to a lot of potential clients about this - is how much does it cost? I'm here to tell you that it can be expensive. I've had new clients tell me they were routinely quoted $3000 to $4,000 for legal fees to set up a new website.

- And what about keeping your site legally compliant? There would be additional fees from time to time to keep your site current with new legal developments.

So, bottom line, an Internet attorney is ALWAYS your best option, but is it within your budget? This isn't a problem for the big guys on the web who rely heavily on their law firms, but it's a real problem for the smaller entrepreneurs.

Option 2: Purchase (or "Borrow") Cheap, Downloadable, Cookie Cutter Forms. Do You Really Want To Do That?

If you don't have the budget to hire an Internet attorney, then you might be tempted to purchase some of those downloadable, cookie cutter forms from the Internet.

You know, the generic forms that are all basically the same – one size fits all.

But if you think about it you've probably got some lingering doubts about these forms:

- Does the generic form really fit my specific requirements of my site?

- Do you know how to use the forms?

- Do you even know who created the darn things?

- What's their background? I even know of a site where the attorney spokesperson doesn't even practice Internet law, but he's the spokesperson who sells these downloadable forms.

- And are these forms ever updated? Just to name a few.

So, do you have confidence that these downloadable forms are a real legal solution you can have confidence in?

Option 3: FTCGuardian.com – Begin With FREE download, Website Legal Compliance Blueprint www.ftcguardian.com/blueprint

I'd like to tell you my story.

It all began back in the late '80s.

That's when my software law practice was really humming, and I was working with a lot of clients who required relatively complex legal documents:

- Enterprise Software License Agreements,
- Software Distribution Agreements,
- Software Reseller Agreements,
- Private label Reseller Agreements,
- Software Publishing Agreements, and
- Software OEM Agreements.

I was using the cut and paste method.

And it was driving me crazy!

Why? The documents were too complex for cut and paste to be efficient.

I was always looking for the right form.

And even then, I was always worried about leaving something out of the transaction I was working on because the form I was using was based on another transaction.

So, in the early 90's, I bought a book on document automation. It was all about how to create a system that would automate the process of document creation.

It wasn't about forms and templates.

It was about how to build in logic so that the system would be "intelligent". A system that would enable me to create logic pathways, such as:

- Is the license non-exclusive? or
- Is it exclusive?

And depending on my selection of the option, it would provide additional relevant options, pathways, and decisions to make regarding the finished document.

The result would be a customized document – a document that once the system was programmed with all of my knowledge regarding an OEM agreement (for example), would include all of the relevant options and related clauses.

Bottom line, it would be a bear to program. But once programmed, it would almost be a magic tool.

But, I'm not a programmer, even though I had a Fortran IV course in grad school. I knew my limits.

So, I used the merge text functionality in a word processor. It enabled me to create question with a "yes" or "no" answer. And you could write a logic statement based on simple yes-no logic:

- "yes" would include the paragraph, and
- "no" would not include it.

I created a complex OEM agreement. It took a long time.

And it worked. But, there was a huge draw-back. The number of clauses was so large that the system was too unwieldy to be efficient to modify and to work with.

And later, a software client suggested that a database-centric approach would be a significant improvement. The clauses would be loaded in a database and external logic would determine whether to add the paragraph and where it would be located within the document.

Technically, it would be a system that incorporated methodology known as "rule-based document assembly".

So, I designed the system, and he programmed it.

7 Tragic (Legal) Mistakes That Can Get Your Bank Accounts Frozen By The FTC Leaving You Penniless...

The result (after the difficult and time-consuming process of creating the logic and loading the database) was almost like magic!

It was like replacing an axe with a power saw.

It almost made document creation fun!

Much later, another client suggested that I make a product out of my rule-based document assembly system.

So, in 1996, we created a website and added downloadable software and the database of legal documents designed for software companies.

Finally, in 2000, we ported the system to my website so that all the processing would occur on the server, and the finished document would be delivered by email.

It was one of the first systems incorporating what is known today as "software as a service" or "SaaS".

For users, there was no software to download and install. The software remained on the server. All a user had to do was:
- simply login with an ID and password,
- select a document from the menu,
- answer a series of questions,
- then with the click of a Submit button, assemble a document on the fly for immediate download.

The output was a .txt file that could be copied into any word processor for further editing.

And most important, the output was:
- a customized document,
- with all the clauses numbered and formatted as they should be.

And we're still using this software today.

Before the tsunami of new laws for websites began in 2009, I could see it coming. So, I created packages of documents designed for Internet marketers and online entrepreneurs for:
- website legal compliance,
- intellectual property protection
- customer agreements, and
- channel marketing agreements (marketing via affiliates and resellers).

Later, in 2013, I realized that something very important was missing.

It became clear to me that it wasn't just about documents. It was also about understanding what I call the *"Rules of the Road"* and *"Easy-To-Understand Strategies"*.

Documents alone without:
- understanding how to use them, and
- how to operate an online business legally,

was just *half* a legal solution!

So, I created Rules of the Road Tutorials and Easy-To-Understand Strategies in the form of:

7 Tragic (Legal) Mistakes That Can Get Your Bank Accounts Frozen By The FTC Leaving You Penniless...

- easy 5-minute videos, and
- quick-start cheat sheets.

I boiled the rules and strategies down to their essence so they would be quick and easy to understand and follow. And this dynamic combination of document packages, Rules of The Road Tutorials, and Easy-To-Understand strategies accomplishes my *Mission Statement*:

- To *empower* you with a Simple Online Legal Solution...
- so you can be as successful as you want, and to grow your online businesses, as fast as you want...
- with the *confidence* that you're as legally protected as the Big Guys who can afford to hire expensive law firms,
- but without the high cost!

Tip: A complete online legal solution, absolutely, positively must include both:
- intelligent software to create customized legal documents, and
- Rules of the Road Tutorials and Easy-To-Understand Strategies..

If it doesn't, then it's not a complete solution!

Conclusion

The Tragic Mistakes

There are a lot of tragic legal Mistakes, particularly with FTC compliance. I've chosen what I believe are the Top 7 Tragic Mistakes with FTC compliance. The ones you absolutely, positively need to avoid. Right now.

Additional Tragic Mistakes are presented in the Appendices. They're important, but they didn't make the cut for my Top 7 list.

The tragic Mistakes presented in this book are not presented to frighten. Instead, they should be perceived as issues that responsible online marketers should deal with.

For protection of your online business, yes.

For the protection of your personal assets, definitely yes!

But also, for a statement reflecting the best practices that you follow in your online business.

Don't fall into the trap of thinking that these tragic Mistakes only affect the Big Guys. They apply to all online businesses - to Internet veterans and to new travelers on the road to online success.

And they have one thing in common – all of them can be avoided!

And remember this: if you don't take action to avoid the Mistakes, then you've made a conscious decision to put yourself, your personal assets, and your family, at risk.

All you need is the commitment to do it the right way. Plus, the necessary documents and information to guide you.

And if you do it the right way, your journey along the road to online success will be a much safer and more rewarding one. Trust me on that!

Appendices

Tragic Mistakes With The FTC That Didn't Make The Top 7 List

7 Tragic (Legal) Mistakes That Can Get Your Bank Accounts Frozen By The FTC Leaving You Penniless...

Appendix 1

FTC Accelerates Crackdown On Fake News Sites

We've all seen headlines in search results like this one – "XYZ Exposed: Miracle Diet or Scam". And perhaps we actually believed there was objective reporting or unbiased commentary behind the headline. But after reading the web page, it was clear that the headline was just a clever way to catch your attention and lure you to a sales page with an aggressive sales pitch.

The Federal Trade Commission (FTC) has seen these headlines too, and the FTC doesn't think they're clever at all. In fact, the FTC believes they constitute deceptive and unfair trade practices, as indicated by the FTC's accelerated crackdown on affiliates of a popular diet drink with aggressive weight loss claims.

Modus Operandi

The modus operandi of these sites was to start with attention grabbing headlines such as the one listed above and these additional ones - "News 6 News Alerts," "Health News Health Alerts," or "Health 5 Beat News."

7 Tragic (Legal) Mistakes That Can Get Your Bank Accounts Frozen By The FTC Leaving You Penniless...

The sites presented what appeared to be a skeptical commentator who raises the question of whether the diet drink is really effective. The commentator appeared to be objective; however, after a few paragraphs the commentator would conclude that use of the diet drink would result in a 25-pound weight loss in 4 weeks - all this without changing diet or exercise according to the FTC. The prices for the supplement ranged between $70 and $100.

The FTC's Claims

When the FTC originally initiated law suits against these sites, Charles Harwood, Deputy Director of the FTC's Bureau of Consumer Protection stated: "We are alleging that nearly everything about these Web sites is false and deceptive". In addition, the FTC pointed out that the defendants aggressively promoted the deceptive ads by spending millions of dollars for placement on high volume websites resulting in millions of views by consumers and substantial sales.

Specifically, the FTC contended that the offending sites:

o failed to disclose their material relationships involving the payment of affiliate commissions with the merchants of the products;

o failed to produce independent tests to support the claims made prior to public dissemination;

o included a section of "consumer comments" that were completely fabricated;

- used infringing logos of reputable media outlets such as ABC, Fox News, CNN and Consumer Reports to give the false impression of credibility; and
- misappropriated the image of a French reporter for use on the sites.

The Settlements

The cases brought by the FTC were against six affiliates of the merchant that manufactured and supplied the weight loss supplement.

In the settlements, the defendants agreed that they will permanently cease their allegedly deceptive practice of using fake news websites. In addition, the settlements require that the defendants cease making deceptive claims about their other products, including work-at-home schemes and penny auctions which most of them promoted.

The big hammer in the settlements included fines in an aggregate amount which represented the affiliate commissions the defendants received through their fake news sites.

These settlement results clearly indicate that the FTC aggressively pursued every dollar they could under the circumstances (the final amounts left most of them with few real assets, if any):

- one defendant's $2.5 million judgment was suspended when he paid $280,000 and recorded a $39,500 lien on his home;

- another defendant's fine of $204,000 was suspended pending the payment of $13,000 plus the proceeds from the sale of a BMW automobile, and

- still another defendant was suspended pending the payment of almost $80,000 over a 3 year period.

Conclusion

The take-aways from these cases include:

- fake news sites are virtually guaranteed to get you sued by the FTC,

- ditto for fake testimonials or user comments,

- diet supplements of any kind are high on the FTC's radar screen for regulatory scrutiny,

- the FTC is serious about enforcing its guidelines that affiliates are required to conspicuously disclose the fact that they are paid commissions for endorsements,

- consistent with the FTC's long-standing policy, advertising claims should be substantiated prior to public dissemination.

The FTC continues to make it absolutely clear that the days of the "Wild, Wild West" on the Internet, when it was open season on deceptive marketing practices, are clearly over for good.

Appendix 2

Blockbuster FTC Settlement! Jesse Willms Agrees To $359 Million Settlement For Deceptive Marketing Practice Claims

In a recent settlement, the Federal Trade Commission (FTC) made it clear that deceptive website legal documents, particularly those that support "free" offers, will not be tolerated.

According to the FTC, the deceptive marketing schemes employed by the defendants netted over $450 million in sales. The result - the FTC came down hard on the defendants, with one individual defendant giving up all the money in his bank accounts, his house, automobile, and other personal property.

The takeaways from this settlement provide clear guidelines for all Internet marketers, particularly those who with sites that use "Free" offers as a lure for upsells to provide recurring revenue, or so-called "continuity" websites.

The Marketing Schemes

The offers were for products with broad market appeal, including weight-loss pills, teeth whiteners, health supplements, work-at-home options, access to government grants, free credit reports, and penny auctions.

A key factor in the marketing scheme was the lure of "free" offers, including "free" trials. Consumers were often charged a monthly fee, typically $79.95, plus additional monthly recurring fees for "bonus" offers and upsells.

Another key factor in the marketing scheme was significant leverage through affiliates – who drove traffic to the websites with the offers through widespread use of banner ads, pay-per-click ads, pop-ups, and unsolicited email. Affiliates were paid commissions for the sales resulting from traffic sent to the offering websites.

The Devil Is In The Details

Neither of the above key factors in the marketing scheme are per se illegal. The problem, according to the FTC, is in the details of how the defendants used the key factors to deceive consumers in violation of the FTC Act.

The following checklist summarizes the deceptive elements alleged by the FTC.

o Misrepresentations About "Free", "Risk-Free", and "Bonus". The primary lures for consumers were the "Free" offers. The defendants induced consumers to provide their credit or debit card information by falsely promising that the product or service could be acquired on a "free" or "risk-free" trial basis while only paying a nominal shipping and handling fee. Some offers represented that the consumer would receive a product or service as a "bonus" for simply signing up. In fact, consumers were charged for products or services that they didn't know about or had not agreed to purchase, and in some cases the charges were recurring on a monthly basis. The process for cancelling these charges or obtaining refunds involved separate time-consuming phone calls and other steps designed to significantly increase difficulty.

o Failure to Disclose, or Deceptive Disclosure of, Additional Charges. Despite the "free" offers, there were additional charges. In some cases there was no disclosure of additional charges. In many cases, there were disclosures regarding the additional charges, but the disclosures were not in a clear and understandable manner. Additional terms were buried in a separate "terms and conditions" page loaded with "lengthy, legalistic fine print" that was not accessible from the ordering page. Consumers were not required to click on an "I Agree" button to indicate acceptance with the "terms and conditions" page.

o Deceptive Refund Policies. Another significant lure for consumers were generous refund offers. Promises included "100% Satisfaction Guarantee", "Risk Free Guarantee", and "Easy Money Back Guarantee... Just Follow the 3 Easy Steps". In fact, refund requests were denied, or if promised, they were never issued. In many cases consumers had to resort to complaints to law enforcement or the Better Business Bureau to actually get a refund.

7 Tragic (Legal) Mistakes That Can Get Your Bank Accounts Frozen By The FTC Leaving You Penniless...

- o Failure to Disclose, or Deceptive Disclosure of, Limitations on Cancellations and Refunds. Despite the refund offers, there were limitations on cancellations and refunds which were either not disclosed or not adequately disclosed.

- o False and Unsubstantiated Efficacy Claims. The defendants did not possess or rely upon a reasonable basis to substantiate their advertising claims on banner ads approved by the defendants for use by affiliate marketers.

- o False Celebrity and Other Endorsements. The defendants displayed images of celebrities on their websites without permission and falsely represented that these celebrities endorsed the defendants' products. In addition, logos for prominent news entities were displayed with statements such as "Featured On" and "As Seen On TV", when in fact none of these entities endorsed or positively reported on any of the products.

- o Evading Risk Management Rules to Obtain Merchant Accounts. The defendants submitted inaccurate financial information to merchant banks in order to retain or obtain merchant credit card processing accounts.

The Settlement

The settlement included substantial payments by the defendants from the sale of business and personal assets. In addition, the defendants' were enjoined for future violations of the deceptive practices discussed above.

Finally, regarding their affiliates, the defendants were ordered:

- to disclose to all affiliates that engaging in deceptive practices would result in immediate termination, and

- to monitor affiliate activities monthly for violations.

Conclusion – Important Settlement Takeaways

Most of the takeaways from this settlement are obvious egregious violations. However, there are three takeaways that are perhaps not so obvious, but which are significant for Internet marketers:

- reliance on disclosures or disclaimers in website legal documents alone is not enough to avoid liability; in this case there were disclosures regarding additional charges and refunds limitations, but they were buried in the "fine print", and therefore, they were not clearly and conspicuously disclosed in order to avoid consumer deception;

- even if disclosures are clearly and conspicuously disclosed, using "Free" offers as a lure for upsells, particularly if the upsells involve recurring revenue (continuity plans), will always be a red flag issue, and therefore, attract close scrutiny by the FTC; and

- using affiliates to advertise and drive traffic for sales does not absolve an Internet marketer merchant from liability for the affiliates' deceptive practices;

monitoring of affiliate marketing practices and termination of offending affiliates is required.

Appendix 3

FTC's Settlement With Google Provides Game Changing Internet Privacy Regulations

You've certainly heard about Google's highly promoted BUZZ service which is designed to compete directly with Twitter by offering much of Twitter's basic functionality with a Facebook-like platform including location data integrated into Gmail. What you may not have heard is that the Federal Trade Commission (FTC) recently made BUZZ the poster child for the FTC's effort to show that the old tried and true privacy protection methodology is now not enough.

Once again, the FTC has upped the ante for privacy requirements, and all websites are expected to comply with the new game changing regulations, or face the consequences.

The FTC's Allegations

On March 30, 2011, the FTC announced a proposed consent order regarding Google's BUZZ service. According the FTC, Google had engaged in deceptive practices regarding discrepancies between its privacy policy statements and its actual practices regarding BUZZ.

Google's privacy policy stated in part: "When you sign up for a particular service that requires registration, we ask you to provide personal information. If we use this information in a manner different than the purpose for which it was collected, then we will ask for your consent prior to such use."

When Google launched BUZZ, Google invited its Gmail users to sign-up with two options:

o "Sweet! Check out Buzz", or
o "Nah, go to my inbox".

The FTC alleged that both of these options were deceptive. The "Sweet" option was allegedly deceptive because users were not clearly informed that the identities of certain of their email recipients would be made public by default. The FTC claimed this was contrary to Google's promise to obtain consent for new information uses and also in violation of Google's requirements in its self-certified participation in the US-EU Safe Harbor program.

The "Nah" option was allegedly deceptive because users were unwittingly enrolled in certain parts of BUZZ despite selecting "Nah".

The Game Changers

As part of the proposed settlement, Google is required to implement a comprehensive privacy program with very specific mandated requirements and to undergo privacy audits over the next twenty years. This requirement is not new. The FTC has historically signaled its expectations through consent orders with similar requirements.

What's new, and certainly game changing, are the following.

o Covered Information. Up to now, privacy regulations has focused on "personal information" that may be used to identify an individual person. From now on, the focus will be on "covered information" which the FTC construes to cover additional elements including screen names, location data, and lists of contacts.

o Privacy by Design. Generally, privacy by design is a holistic approach where privacy compliance is designed physically into systems from their inception, rather than waiting to address compliance the end of the design process or separately through a published privacy policy. Although at this time there is scant information regarding privacy design specifics, a safe bet is that privacy by design will involve pop-up or interstitial messaging regarding the use and sharing of covered information at the time a user discloses information or opts in to a specific program. This is in stark contrast to the current practice of providing all such messaging in a separately published privacy policy.

Conclusion

With the proposed BUZZ settlement, the FTC has aggressively raised the bar in terms of privacy requirements for all online businesses. In essence, the FTC settlements have created "common law" regarding privacy, and websites that fail to comply do so at their peril.

Expect more specific information regarding the game changers in the form of additional suits and settlements by the FTC in the near future.

Appendix 4

The FTC Begins Crackdown On Behavioral Ads - Is Your Site In The Cross Hairs?

On March 14, 2011, the Federal Trade Commission (FTC) announced its first behavioral advertising settlement. If your website collects behavioral data or serves behavioral ads – either directly or indirectly through the use of behavioral ad vendors – you need to understand and comply with the FTC's notice and choice principles, or suffer the consequences.

What Is Behavioral Advertising?

Behavioral ads are based on anonymous data collected on how a user's computer browses the Internet, including websites visited, searches made, and content read. This data is used to create a behavioral profile that is linked to a specific demographic. The ads seen by the computer's user are tailored to the user's interests resulting in significantly increased relevancy and sales.

Contextual ads, in contrast to behavioral ads, are based solely on the content of the specific website page the user is viewing. Because contextual ads are generally not as relevant to the user's interests as behavioral ads, contextual ads are less effective, and therefore less profitable.

Although behavioral data is essentially anonymous when collected, the FTC and privacy advocates are concerned that the amount and depth of some data could lead to personal identification of users. In addition, even if users are not personally identified, the enhanced data about them could rise to the level of an invasion of privacy.

The Chitka Settlement

In 2009, the FTC issued a staff report on behavioral advertising that explained the FTC's principles regarding behavioral data. The FTC believes that its deceptive and a violation of the FTC Act to fail to provide to consumers proper notice and opt-out choice regarding the collection of behavioral data. The FTC's settlement with Chitka, Inc. is the first settlement based on these principles.

Chitka is an intermediary between advertisers and websites that serve ads for the advertisers. To collect behavioral data, Chitka passes a cookie on users' computers and then uses the cookie to tracks the users' online behavior.

The FTC alleged in its Complaint that for over two years Chitka advised consumers that if they wanted to opt out of behavioral tracking they could click on a button titled "opt out". Clicking the button would generate a message that read "you are opted out". The catch according to the FTC is that the opt out lasted only for ten days, and then new cookies would be passed to consumers' computers resulting in tracking of behavioral data for serving behavioral ads.

In its settlement with the FTC, Chitka agreed to:

- o delete all identifiable user information collected during the ineffective opt out period,

- o provide consumers with a new opt out mechanism that lasts for at least five years, and

- o notify consumers whose opt out was ineffective to opt out again.

Chitka also agreed to a notice and opt out procedure that could be interpreted as a blue print for what the FTC believes is generally required for all sites that collect behavioral data. This procedure includes:

- o A message on the home page that reads "we collect information about your activities on certain websites to send you targeted advertisements. To opt out of [our] targeted ads, click here."

- o The "here" link points to an opt out page where the user is notified that opt out means the information would not be used for behavioral ads, the status of the opt out (in or out), and that opt out is limited to a specific browser and should be repeated if another browser is used.

- o A link on any behavioral ad that reads "Opt Out?", and that provides text when the users' cursor hovers over the ad that reads "Opt Out of Targeted Ads". The Opt Out? link would point to the opt out page described above.

Conclusion

The Chitka settlement clearly establishes that the FTC believes it's a deceptive practice under the FTC Act to fail to provide notice and opt out choice regarding behavioral

ads. What's more important is that the notice and opt out procedure agreed to in the settlement may be a clear indication of the specific procedure that the FTC requires for compliance.

About Chip Cooper, Esq.

Law Practice
- Of Counsel, Jones & Haley, P.C. Atlanta
- Internet, Software and SaaS Attorney
- Intellectual Property Protection and Transactions
- Content, Software and SaaS Licensing and Distribution Transactions
- Website Legal Compliance

- Mergers & Acquisitions
- Adjunct Professor, Software Law, Wake Forest University School of Law, 20 years.

Education
- Wake Forest University, BA
- Wake Forest University School of Law, Juris Doctor
- University of Georgia, Terry College of Business

Martindale.com - AV Rating (highest peer rating)

Published Author
- *Law and The Software Marketer, How To Develop a Legal Protection Game Plan*, Prentice-Hall
- *Software Distribution, How To Develop a Successful Marketing Plan,* SoftChannel Press

Law Firm Website
- http://www.corplaw.net/

FTC Compliance Website
- www.ftcguardian.com/

For more information for Chip Cooper to appear as a speaker at your event or to present a webinar based on this book contact:

> **Chip Cooper**
> **Jones & Haley, P.C.**
> **South Terraces, Suite 170**
> **115 Perimeter Center Place**

Atlanta, GA 30346-1238
770-664-8555
chip@ftcguardian.com
LinkedIn: www.linkedin.com/in/chipcooper
Skype: chip.cooper.esq

More About The Author

Keith Okano
President, Bridgeway Software, Inc.

"I've worked with many attorneys over 30+ years in the software and technology business and overall Chip is the best. He is expert in his knowledge of software contracts and my trusted counsel not only helping us close business, but also in ensuring we have the knowledge needed to manage and develop our company according to our needs and desires.

Chip does this not by simply offering "data," but taking the time to know and to understand us. Therefore he offers us more than advice, it is wisdom. Chip is a key part of my advisory team and I look forward to working with him for many years (and if necessary many companies) into the future."

Maurizio Taverna
CTO, Mylaensys, LLC

"I recently asked Chip to work on intellectual property, licensing, SaaS agreements and website legal compliancy. I found Chip to be friendly, professional and a person to work with. I would recommend Chip to anyone looking for

legal expertise to address the issues for legal compliance and protection."

Klaus K. Obermeier
Big Data scientist, NLP expert, Artificial Intelligence professional

"Chip is a no-nonsense attorney that helped us during an $11 Million forward triangular merger and negotiated a large cash component. He has a Colombo-style inquisitiveness that gets to the bottom of every deal. Great to have him on your side."

Bill Needle
Intellectual Property Attorney, Mediator, Arbitrator & Special Master

"I've known Chip as an attorney for over 20 years. Chip is a top notch SaaS attorney and software attorney who has a depth of knowledge not only of the law, but also of the software and Internet industry that's reflected in his legal documents and negotiations. He has a knack for resolving complex legal issues in SaaS and software transactions from a business perspective.

Chip is also a BBQ connoisseur who has been my mentor as a fellow Certified BBQ Judge at several Memphis in May World Championship BBQ Cooking Contests."

Alex Eckelberry
Technology Entrepreneur And Executive

"Chip is a world-class expert in a broad range of issues. He has worked with us many times on software contracts, IP and other issues. He is always fair in his pricing, and is a highly ethical man of real integrity. I would recommend him without hesitation."

Tom Johnson
Owner, PaperSoft

"We've engaged Chip for our Software License Agreements for years. He's very knowledgeable and gets to the point quickly. He always does a great job."

Made in the USA
Charleston, SC
20 December 2014